Commentary On Genesis

Volume 1

Discussions In Scripture Series

A Creationist Commentary

By Pastor Steven Waldron

Copyright 2021 by Steven Waldron.

Published 2021.

Printed in the United States of America.

All rights reserved.

No portion of this book may be reproduced, stored in a retrieval system, or transmitted in any form or by any means – electronic, mechanical, photocopy, recording, scanning, or other – except for brief quotations in critical reviews or articles, without the prior written permission of the author.

ISBN 978-1-950647-47-7

Cover image canstockphoto 4243100

Publishing assistance by BookCrafters, Parker, Colorado.
www.bookcrafters.net

An Introduction

THIS IS NOT A MODERN TYPE of Biblical Commentary. Rather, it hearkens back to a time of Scriptural discussions on a popular level from a bygone era. It is an attempt to lift out of Scripture the truths God intended, both in the immediate context and in an applicatory sense. It also does not attempt to answer every question and nuance that Scripture presents. On the essentials it is absolute, such as the Deity of Jesus, monotheism, salvation, holiness, and the character of God. But there are certain ancillary things that very good men disagree on. Paul spoke of days and meats as being some of those issues in Romans 14. According to John 21, the early Church had a rumor that John would not die until Jesus would come back. So, there was latitude on certain things in the early Church. And such there should be today. There is an old saying, "In the essentials unity, in the non-essentials liberty, in all things charity." Now determining what is essential is paramount. God put it like this in Deuteronomy 29:29, "The secret things belong unto the LORD our God: but those things which are revealed belong unto us and to our children for ever, that we may do all the words of this law." Major, essential doctrines will be presented, with other views sometimes offered, and occasionally refuted. Certain issues, such as the identity of the sons of God in Genesis, will be looked at from various viewpoints, but a definitive conclusion may not be proffered. So, we will be discussing Holy Scripture. There is no higher or more important level of discussion that we can have. Oh, that Scripture was on every lip and tongue throughout the world!

Matthew Henry, Thomas Scott, Matthew Poole, Charles Spurgeon, Charles Wesley, and D.L. Moody are among Biblical expositors in times past that would have used a similar style of engagement with Holy Writ. Truth will be presented. However, it may not always be buttressed with the full weight of apologetic argumentation. This present series seeks to be a truthful, honest handling of God's Holy Word in reverence and great care. But it intends on being eminently readable as well. Something to be read enjoyably, as well as a reference work. All evidence for every viewpoint by necessity will not be given. Breadcrumbs may be dropped, handfuls on purpose, to lead to a deeper discovery of truth.

I would be remiss if I did not mention the great mentors and teachers God has so graciously imparted into my life. Dr. Samuel Latta, the great Missionary Evangelist was my Pastor. He died when I was writing this, in the summer of 2019. He will be sorely missed, not just by me, but by the world at large. His passion for Divine Truth is exhilarating. His father, Thomas Latta - Church Planter and Bible expositor nonpareil, had a deep and lasting impact on my life. Sister Ruby Martin of Jackson College of Ministries, and her love of Scripture, was infectious. Pastor Thomas Craft, Dr. David Bernard, Pastor Darrell Johns, Pastor David Reever, Rev. Alan Oggs, Pastor Jonathan Urshan, Pastor Paul Mooney, Pastor Nathaniel Wilson, Pastor Johnny Godair, Pastor Larry Booker, and Rev. O.C. Marler have all sharpened the sword of Scripture in my life in various ways, and for that I am forever grateful. Other ministries and books too countless and laborious to name form a tapestry in my life. The veil of blue, purple, scarlet, cherubim's, and fine twined linen has been sewn warp and woof into my life through them. Without them, and how God used them, my life would in some sense be incomplete. Complete in Jesus yes, but God used them as well. Helpful resources will be mentioned as are deemed appropriate.

The goal is to have a truthful look at each passage of Scripture. Of the making of books there is no end according to Solomon. The world itself could not contain the books that should be written about

Jesus. So, it is impossible to flesh each nugget from every jot and tittle of Scripture. Truth, and God's essential revelation is the desired goal. "How can I understand except some man teach me" was a paraphrased cry of the Ethiopian Eunuch. We should study to show ourselves approved unto God, rightly dividing the word of truth.

The Scripture is the mind of God. It has been with God throughout all eternity. He has graciously revealed and preserved it to mankind. Within its pages are life. They testify of Jesus. What greater thing is there to discuss? So, pull up a chair, and with prayerful, reverent, holy awe, let us see how we can apply God's revealed will to our lives, shall we?

I will not follow current grammatical guidelines concerning capitalization of certain sacred subjects. I will capitalize what I feel is sacred, regardless of current conventions of English. That is my prerogative.

Genesis Background

GENESIS MEANS "BEGINNING." It shows the beginning of all things in this material world. Space, time, and life are all presented here. I am a six-day creationist. I believe this is what Scripture teaches. I have friends who are not. The dates that will be used during this discussion will be basically from Ussher, with help from Floyd Nolen Jones, Reese, and Lloyd. We will discuss as we go, why I believe Scripture teaches six-day creationism, and some of the other theories Christians believe.

All human history goes back to Genesis 1. God has revealed to us where we came from, His ultimate intentions for us, His original intent, and how sin dreadfully made everything wrong. He even shows the process of the "Fall." All Spiritual and Scientific laws are found here in Creation.

The theory of Evolution destroys our connections with the past and with God. Are we in the image of a bacteria or God? Does the world have purpose, or is all just random chance? How can we know where we are going if we do not know where we came from? Is there a sense of meaning?

The literal interpretation of the Book of Genesis is consistent with reality. It is what we see when we look around, whether biologically, geologically, morally, or astronomically. Everything fits perfectly with Scripture. In Genesis we see a beneficent, merciful, Holy God. We see creation as good and very good. Genesis begins with perfection. Our heart constantly cries back for Eden. Utopian schemes and dreams, Jungian archetypes, tragedies, and redemption of Romanticism are all echoes back to Eden. Our susceptibility to platitudes, demagoguery, and the cry of liberty, equality, and fraternity are the fallen human state trying to fix what is wrong, what went wrong at Eden. Unfortunately, our lens is tainted and skewed. And we are powerless in ourselves to fix it. Only the Creator can fix creation. We tend to build towers of Babel.

Genesis tells of the worldwide Deluge, which explains geology and fossils. Babel records the origin of languages. Genesis 10 tells of the dispersion of Nations - the 70 Nations the Jews speak of. In Genesis, 2,000 years of human history is recorded. Paradise is lost, but the plan for Paradise to be regained is implemented. Genesis is truly the foundation for the remainder of Scripture, and life itself. The past is prologue. It shows where sin and death originally came from. Death, as theistic evolutionists erroneously teach, was not God's method for perfecting the world. Death came by sin and made the perfect creation imperfect.

The goodness and severity of God is seen in Genesis. Goodness, in a perfect creation, with blessing for all. Judgment, in a worldwide Deluge which destroyed almost everything. Goodness, in future redemption being foretold. Judgment, with the scattering at Babel and the destruction of Sodom and Gomorrah. Mankind continually wrestles with the hues of the Garden of Eden. An insatiable quest for knowledge. A hunger for justice and righteousness. A perfect world, which is just out of grasp, colored by our sinful nature. It seems to get worse not better. Entropy, the 2nd Law of Thermodynamics, or as Theologians call it, "the Curse and the Fall," has entered in the created world.

We want eternal life. Our heart longs for the missing piece. And what is missing is Him. He fulfills all. Mankind has a touch of the supernal in him. Something beyond the material. Cartesian dualism not Hobbian rationalism rules the day. Conscience, intellect, discovery, awe, beauty, all non-evolutionary attributes, are yet somehow still a part of us. We know things are imperfect. Genesis explains how, why, and what. Let us discuss this and talk about it, and live for Jesus, until that day when we shall know as we are now known.

Data for Genesis: 50 Chapters, 1,533 Verses, 38,262 Words (From Laurence Vance, whom I have found to be the most accurate in detailing various details of Scripture).

Eleven hundred and fifty-six verses begin with the word "and," there are 1,385 verses of history, 148 questions, 56 prophecies, 123 verses of fulfilled prophecy, and 23 verses of unfulfilled prophecy. Chapter 16 is the shortest chapter in Genesis, Chapter 24 is the longest. Chapter 16 has 16 verses, and Chapter 32 has 32 verses. There are 106 commands, 71 promises, 326 predictions, and 95 direct messages from God. All this information comes from the *Dake Study Bible*, that voluminous fount of meticulous research by Finis Dake. I know of no one who has taken the time to check the accuracy of each of his findings, though it is quite possible someone has. It is listed for information's sake, and I cannot vouch for its veracity in every detail.

Dr. Henry Morris in the *Morris Study Bible* lists 200 quotes or allusions to Genesis in the New Testament. He also observes:

1) All Books of the NT except Philemon, 1 John, and 3 John contain allusions to Genesis. He is wrong. 1 John speaks of Cain.
2) Forty-three chapters of Genesis have a quotation or citation in the NT (Genesis chapters 20, 24, 34, 36, 40, 43, 44 are the 7 not mentioned).
3) More than half of the 200 NT allusions are from Genesis 1-11, and 63 of them are from Genesis 1-3.
4) Fourteen of the citations are to the Flood chapters of Genesis 6-8. 58 are references to Abraham.
5) Twenty-five of the references are made by Jesus Himself. It is His most quoted Old Testament book.

Genesis comes from the Greek language and means "origin." The Hebrew title is "Bereshith" which is "In the beginning" (Hebrews title the Biblical Books normally on the first word or phrase of the Book).

Eleven separate units begin with the word "generations," and many use this as a natural way to outline the Book.

Moses wrote Genesis. Jesus had much to say on the Mosaic authorship of the Pentateuch. It was written around 1490 B.C. in the Wilderness wanderings of Israel.

Recommended Books on Genesis:

The Genesis Flood by Henry Morris and John C. Whitcomb

The Genesis Record by Henry Morris

Genesis in the Through the Bible Commentary Series by J. Vernon McGee

Be Basic by Warren W. Wiersbe

Books by Bill Cooper and the Creation Science Movement U.K.

Exploring Genesis by John Phillips

Books by Ken Ham

In the Beginning by Walt Brown

The Evolution Handbook by Vance Ferrell

Creation Vs. Evolution by Arlo C. Moehlenpah

Not all of these are commentaries per se. Some deal with Creation and the issues surrounding that.

Chapter 1

"In the beginning God created the heaven and the earth."
Genesis 1:1

TEN WORDS SHOWING THE BEGINNING of time (beginning), power, created (force), God's Heavenly Kingdom (the heaven), and the physical world (earth). What was before the beginning? God. In Job 38:7 it says the sons of God shouted for joy at creation, so they were already there (this is speaking of angels; b'nai Elohim). God had no beginning. Eternal has no start. We only posit the question because in our finite minds, and our environment, living things have a beginning.

Some speculate about Multiverses and multi-dimensionality. Since God can do exceedingly abundantly above all that we can ask or think, God must be playing quintillion to the septillion power multi-dimensional chess. A near infinite number of worm-holed existences, so the postulation goes. Maybe, maybe not. I do not want to get into an Anselm type ontological discussion here, but some questions naturally arise. Did Jesus' blood cover any beings in these other places? Were there other creatures? Do they go to the same Heaven as we? One part of me says it is the height of hubris to assume we are the only things before or after Genesis 1:1 besides angels. But something else tells me it opens a New Testament (NT) can of worms if we assume there is or was other Multiverses in other dimensions with living beings not even remotely mentioned in Scripture. Does God have multiple manifestations of His Throne for these other worlds and places? Multiple manifestations of hell or eternal punishment? And this does not even posit the supposed "Earth's" constantly being discovered in our Universe. Privileged Planet, the great Creationist DVD answers this question for me in many ways. And the answer is in the negative, at least in our current Universe.

This brings us to pre-Adamite civilization. The theory goes something like this: How the earth got to be without form and void, and with water and darkness on it was the result of the satanic flood. This is where dinosaur fossils come from. Isaiah 14, Jeremiah 4, and Ezekiel 28 are referenced to try and buttress this. A gap is inserted between Genesis 1:1 and 2. Some try to say the first two or three days of creation are of unlimited time, and the rest, are really 24-hour days. I, for one, do not see it. I have friends who count the Gap theory as one of the major doctrines of Scripture. I do think this is a doctrine, the Gap Theory, where good people can disagree. See Romans 14 on instances Christians disagreeing on some doctrines, as well as Matthew 5:19. There are other New Testament passages, as well.

Mark Twain (Samuel Clemens) may have said it best when he said (paraphrasing) it's not the things that I don't understand in Scripture I'm worried about, it's the things I do understand that I'm concerned about. He was a noted skeptic, by the way.

In our discussion, we are just going to be discussing this time-period and the things plainly taught in Scripture. Speculations of dubious authority will be avoided as pertains to doctrine, but they may be mentioned as the author sees fit. So, let us look at some pertinent passages about the Creation of the World. This is often referred to as Ex Nihilo, or "out of nothing." Some have pointed out there was something, God, in the beginning. But nothing material, for God is a Spirit.

John 1:1-3 reads "In the beginning was the Word, and the Word was with God, and the Word was God. The same was in the beginning with God. All things were made by him; and without him was not anything made that was made."

1 John 1:1, 2 "That which was from the beginning, which we have heard, which we have seen with our eyes, which we have looked

upon, and our hands have handled, of the Word of life; (For the life was manifested, and we have seen it, and bear witness, and shew unto you that eternal life, which was with the Father, and was manifested unto us;)"

Ephesians 1:4 "According as he hath chosen us in him before the foundation of the world, that we should be holy and without blame before him in love:"

Colossians 1:16 "For by him were all things created, that are in heaven, and that are in earth, visible and invisible, whether they be thrones, or dominions, or principalities, or powers: all things were created by him, and for him:"

So, we can see from these few Scriptures that the point of all Creation is Jesus Christ. He is the Creator and Sustainer of the Universe. I tend to think any doctrine and speculation that diminishes Jesus is not a good thing, such as the quintillions of other universes past and present in other dimensions, etc. Scripture clearly focuses on Him. And we are in His image. So, it focuses on His great love and redemption plan for us, to save us from sin.

God is the fourth word of Scripture. He is the Author of Scripture and He is its central focus. He is often described as Omnipotent (all powerful), Omniscient (all knowing), Omnipresent (everywhere present), and Omnibenevolent (all good). He created all that is, "ex nihilo," out of nothing. He did not need to start with anything but Himself. He is self-sufficient. He is a Spirit. He is One. He is not a corporate One, but rather an absolute One. It is said that Monotheism built Western Civilization. Thomas Aquinas among others would say that God's basic essential being is "simple," which means "One with no ancillary parts."

I reject the family model of the trinity. The word "trinity" is nowhere found in Scripture. To say since God is love, and love needs an object, so there must be a multiplicity of persons in the Godhead, denies God of His essential self-sufficiency. If man is in the image of God, man is not three persons, rather one. Yet Jesus Christ is often referred to as God. Jesus is God in the flesh. The Incarnation, the Son of God, God in the flesh.

God's creative power is infinite in Himself. He has no need of anything. All that exists is for His pleasure (Revelation 4:11). God is Elohim, a plural of majesty, an intensive, power, and omnipotence. God is without limitations and hence boundless.

Some would say that matter has always existed. Hence, matter is eternal. Since God is eternal, this would also make matter God. "Nothing comes from nothing" as Parmenides so astutely observed.

The law of Biogenesis says life must come from life. Louis Pasteur disproved abiogenesis and spontaneous generation with his Pasteur Beaker. If matter, which is non-living and hence inorganic, is eternal, whence life? Whence consciousness? What forces acted upon matter to produce life? Static objects stay static unless moved upon by an outside force. And whence these forces? Where did they come from or originate?

Occam's Razor says that the simplest solution which fulfills most, or all the known facts is usually correct. Since everything we see around us corresponds perfectly with Genesis chaps. 1-3, and no other theory of origins is even remotely plausible, Genesis chaps. 1-3 is most likely correct according to Occam's Razor. And with scientific verification abounding, I would say the evidence is incontrovertible that God creating everything as shown in Genesis is absolutely, correct.

Recent creation by a living God in many cases disrupts our sensibilities. Cognitive disruption is a precursor to the discovery of truth in many instances. Because we are biased against a certain view that does not make the facts any less factual. Science tends to reject anything outside of the natural, material word a priori. It is impossible to a materialistic viewpoint. But that is a manmade formulation, something humans have agreed upon in a certain sphere. It does not make it true. I am reminded that when the scientist reaches the highest mountain, they find the theologian sitting there.

God created the heaven and the earth. The KJV is one of the few translations which translates heaven here in the singular. This would be the place of God's throne, while earth would be His footstool. I am assuming the KJV translates this word as singular for a reason(s). Possibly since the other heavens are created later in Genesis 1, and Paul indicates there are only three heavens (2 Corinthians 12), it would bring a contradiction into the text to translate it in the plural.

The KJV translators, as God's Secretaries, knew God has no error in His Word. Possibly it was the way Hebrews (Jewish scholarship) translated the Hebrew word as well. The KJV translators were magisterial in all things pertaining to Hebrew, Greek, and the genre of Biblical Literature. There is a reason it is there. I trust it. There is not the wealth of scholarship available in this area today. It was a particular time and place that was uniquely qualified to have a perfect Bible translated.

Psalm 113:6 "Who humbleth himself to behold the things that are in heaven, and in the earth!"

"The earth abides" is a popular phrase. But the earth had a beginning. God made it. Unique, spectacular, but initially void of life. A molten inner core, which I highly suspect is hell, water beneath as well, tectonic plates, soil on top (a miracle in itself), magma, granite, and other elements and rock. What an amazing sphere hung upon nothing (Job 26:7).

I use Ussher as a primary dating source for Scripture. Yes, I know, I once derisively dismissed Ussher as a Reformation era deluded quack. Until I studied Ussher's incisive reasoning and formulations for his conclusions. His knowledge of ancient history is matchless. It was then I hung my head in shame and admitted he is probably very close to being right if not absolutely. And so, Ussher says Sunday October 23rd 4004 B.C. at 9 a.m. Greenwich Mean time, or midnight in the Garden of Eden, was when the earth was created. Study his original work and disprove him if you must, just do not dismiss him. Only a fool answers a matter before he hears it, Scripture declares. He had over 100 pages of calculations deducing this date, and no less than the inestimable Isaac Newton thought he was very close to being correct.

It is very difficult to discuss Scripture these days. "My Bible says this," "mine reads this way," "did you know the original could be translated this way?" are all phrases that are part and parcel of trying to bring truth into the fray today. For the sake of this discussion, we are going to stick to the King James Version of the Bible, which was done by the most learned company of Biblical scholars to produce a Bible. And they were striving for perfection. Their very existence depended on it, in the theological and governmental fighting that the day dictated. So, since in the making of books there is no end, we will just use this translation for this Commentary. Much like Ussher, I think if you objectively study the KJV translators, you will stand in awe of them and the accuracy of the Bible they produced rather than dismissing it as archaic tripe.

This would have been 1 anno mundi (AM) (after the creation), 710 in the Julian Period (JP), 4004 BC, 3761 BC according to the traditional Jewish Calendar, and 5554 BC in the Septuagint. Many others such as Maimonides and Newton have come up with various dates for creation and would be considered young earth creationists.

Genesis 1:2 "And the earth was without form, and void; and darkness was upon the face of the deep. And the Spirit of God moved upon the face of the waters."

There seems to be no indication of the Gap theory here. It is not necessary. It seems to have been primarily brought into the fray by trying to bridge the widening chasm between science and the Bible. Chalmers, then Pember, then Dake served to popularize it. Willmington and Morris seem to me to do definitive jobs dismantling it. Good men can disagree.

Without form and void seems to be the Artist putting out the clay before fashioning it. Again, nothing indicates a Gap Theory, or a Pre-Adamite world of Lillith, etc. And much militates against it, such as the plain reading of Scripture, and the issue of there being death before the Fall.

Here in verse 2 we have earth, water, and Spirit mentioned. This is quite possibly paradigmatic. We are earth and water, but the Spirit and the Word (the next verse) gives us light and life. Or we are earth, and the water, Spirit, and Word recreates us, i.e. the New Birth of John 3:3-7. Either way it makes for an interesting typological discussion.

To go deeper, we are without our future intent and purpose in our first birth. We are void of the life of God. We are in darkness. But God's Spirit is moving upon us, drawing us ever closer to Him.

Another interesting observation is that God is a Spirit. And this

Spirit is here moving in activity. Some have even said the manifestation of God, the Holy Ghost or Spirit, represents God in activity.

Then we ask why is there water here? To a Gap theorist, the answer is the Pre-Adamite world was destroyed by a flood. Either the destruction was by God for the wickedness of this world, of which we know nothing but speculation, or it was destroyed by Satan, since he comes to steal, kill, and destroy. To a non-Gap theorist, it would just be part of God's creation as found in Genesis 1:1. Creationists wax eloquent on the miraculous properties of water. When God created the earth, part of what that included was water. Or it was part of an act of God not recorded in Scripture, but obviously occurred. I would go with it was part of creation in Genesis 1:1. The Phoenician creation story has waters pouring down from heaven to earth during creation. Maybe this is a fallen recollection of what really occurred.

Genesis 1:3 "And God said, 'Let there be light:' and there was light."

This is the first instance the phrase "and God said" is mentioned. It is used a total of ten times in Genesis 1.

Hebrews 11:3 says, "Through faith we understand that the worlds were framed by the word of God, so that things which are seen were not made of things which do appear."

God is a speaking God. He is verbal. Mankind is still perplexed at language. Trying to explain language from an evolutionary worldview is seemingly impossible. Language has been devolving, not evolving. Ancient languages are more complex than modern languages. The Dispersion at Babel paradigm seems the most plausible explanation and conforms to what we know about language. There are great books on this subject from a Creationist perspective. We can speak, because God speaks, and we are in the image of God. And we are created to respond to God's Word. God has chosen through the foolishness of preaching to save those that believe. Preaching what? The Word. Angels also give attendance to God's Word (Psalm 103:20).

Light here appears from the spoken Word of God. The Word gives illumination. You can see. Light exposes. Scripture declares, "The entrance of thy words giveth light; it giveth understanding unto the simple." (Psalm 119:130). We also read in John 1:5 "And the light shineth in darkness; and the darkness comprehended it not." Light appears in the darkness. God is Light, and in Him is no darkness at all. This particular light appearing is something that is apart from God, however. It is also not associated with the Sun or other astronomical phenomenon, which do not appear until the fourth day.

We can observe from this that when God says something, it happens. His Word is quick and powerful. He is the Creator.

Genesis 1:4 "And God saw the light, that it was good: and God divided the light from the darkness."

Darkness is here seen as the absence of light. Some have carried this to the extreme and said evil, like darkness, does not really exist tangibly, it is merely the absence of light. Some deny the devil and demons because of this. Of course, this is a vast overextrapolation of the Biblical text.

The dividing of light and darkness seems to be another Biblical principle. In 2 Corinthians 6:14b we read, "…and what communion hath light with darkness?" The doctrine of separation and holiness began on the first day of the world. Light and darkness cannot mix.

Genesis 1:5 "And God called the light Day, and the darkness he called Night. And the evening and the morning were the first day."

Calling the light day, and the darkness night has carried over into the present time, just as the 24-hour day and seven-day week has. During the French Revolution, the secular Government changed the week to ten days, recognizing the seven-day week's Biblical origin. The antichrist will seek to change times and seasons. We also observe here that day and night preceded the sun and the moon. The Jews still reckon the day beginning at 6 p.m. predicated on the evening and the morning being the initial Scriptural model.

Notice as well, the change of definition of the word "day" in this verse. Light is day in the beginning of the verse, and darkness is night. Then the entire 24-hour period is referred to as a day in the last part of the verse. This Biblical observation that words sometime have a multiplicity of meaning may be found at various other times in Scripture as well. The so-called Law of First Mention or Reference I find to be very wanting in Scripture. I think it was developed to promulgate certain pet doctrines of some. It is nowhere mentioned in Holy Writ.

So, Day one is here complete. Light has come forth dispelling the darkness. Just as God can provide light without the sun, so can He provide life for the plants on Day three before the sun is created on Day four. And the evening and the morning complete the first day.

Genesis 1:6 "And God said, 'Let there be a firmament in the midst of the waters, and let it divide the waters from the waters.'"

The word "firmament" means expanse. Some feel the expanse is the atmospheric heaven here. Others see the firmament here as the astronomical heaven. If it is astronomical, this would mean there is water in Heaven, the place of God's abode. It would also mean the water in the atmosphere is combined with the waters of the sea for the waters below in verse 7. This would make sense for the hydraulic cycle. On the other hand, flat-earthers would say that waters above would be water in the atmosphere, and the waters below would again be the seas, really with no mention of the water under the earth's surface which is estimated to be three times as much as the water on the surface, and vastly more than that before Noah's Flood. Flat-earthers tend to be geo-centrists as well, saying the stars, sun, moon, etc. all revolve around the earth, and that they are contained within the atmospheric heaven. Revelation does have stars falling from heaven, which unless symbolic of something, would be impossible in a Copernican model. Unless, of course, it is a meteor shower, which we call a falling star, or a comet disintegrating in the atmosphere, an asteroid, etc. The flat-earth theorists, while I applaud their attempt to believe the Word against everything, really stretch credulity, and is unnecessary Biblically.

The Flat Earth theory would say that every photograph of space is wrong. Every photo is intentionally doctored to fit the evidence of the Copernican model, so to speak. I think the CIA says that once a conspiracy reaches 19 people, it can no longer be counted on to be conspiratorial. Evidence will be revealed. But here we have 10,000's of scientists from dozens of different countries, all agreeing at all times even on their death beds to conceal facts. Even to family members. With social media, they could upload their complicity in this vast plot in a moment. Again, it strains credulity. I will proceed in this discussion with a heliocentric, spherical view of the Universe and earth, and share Biblical explanations from that perspective. But the Flat earth view has been increasing exponentially.

So, I would say there is water in Heaven. I am fine with that. Without going into a doctrinal study showing Scriptural indications of that, I will just say the miraculous nature of water in so many life-giving respects fits well with Heaven. Some would say Heaven is a spiritual place. Yes, but the New Jerusalem that comes down from Heaven seems to be material. Jesus carried real Blood to Heaven. Now another explanation of verse 6 and the firmament is that this is speaking of the atmospheric heaven, while later in the chapter, using similar terminology, it is talking about the celestial heaven. That is also plausible under a traditional astronomical view. Going back to water, in the DVD Privileged Planet great detail is given on the miraculous properties of water. And these properties, such as freezing from the top down, among many others, allow for the existence of life. I recommend viewing it.

We also see that division is a key concept early in Genesis. Division of light and dark. Division of waters. Division of Day and Night, Evening and Morning. Later divisions into kinds of various living things are also mentioned. Then an enclosed Garden, separated from the world, for Man and Woman. And the division of what could be consumed, and what could not.

Genesis 1:7 "And God made the firmament, and divided the waters which were under the firmament from the waters which were above the firmament: and it was so."

It is good to remember that verses 6-8 are contiguous. Verse divisions were given for most of the Bible by Robert Etienne (Stephanus) around 1551. This is one reason I like paragraph Bibles. It helps see things as they were originally written (Lamentations, Psalm 119, and possibly some other passages are exceptions). It is difficult to teach and preach from Paragraph Bibles however, and the verse system is very well done. Stephanus did the numbering system for Plato, which is still in use today. The verse system helps in identifying Scriptures. Memorization is enhanced. But when Jesus read from the Synagogue Scroll, or Paul would quote the OT, they did not have the luxury of verses, or even chapters for the most part. So, I read from both paragraph and verse Bibles. I also read from chronological Bibles, which again helps to give me perspective. But they are almost impossible to carry to Church and follow along or teach from.

Stephanus has been much criticized for his verse divisions. Some have jokingly said that he did it while riding a horse, and that every time the horse stepped in a hole, he made a new verse. This is a classic case of assuming scholars of another time were not as enlightened as modern-day students. This is a baneful sort of pride and must be guarded against. Sometimes it is true the new is better, but with evil men and seducers waxing worse and worse deceiving and being deceived, it certainly is not always the case. Selah.

God made the firmament. Is there a difference between "made and create?" Sometimes possibly, but most of the time they are synonymous. What did he make the expanse of? Or is it just void, like darkness is the absence of light? Whatever the vast expanse outer space is made of, it is what God did as being recorded. If it is a void, then it means void. If there are certain particles, then that is what God made here. I guess prevailing scientific opinion, besides the "dark matter" hypothesis needed for the Big Bang theory, is that space between celestial objects is a vacuum.

I love the force of the last four words of verse 7, comprised of 10 letters, single syllables each word, and the longest words are three letters; "and it was so." No muss and fuss with God! He goes to do it and it is done, in orders of magnitude that defy comprehension. I really appreciate the Hubble telescope identifying the vastness of the Universe, as other Near-Earth Platforms do as well. God does monumental, colossal work in an effortless fashion. Just as He said it is finished on the cross, but oh what a price He paid there. He keeps the Universe and each living thing in it functioning smoothly, with no effort on His part. He could do exceedingly abundantly more.

Genesis 1:8 "And God called the firmament Heaven. And the evening and the morning were the second day."

It is obvious that the heaven mentioned here is different from the heaven of Verse 1. This is the astronomical heaven here, later to be filled with wonder.

This, according to Ussher, completes Monday, October 24th 4004 B.C. It also completes the 2nd 24-hour day that existed with darkness and light, night, and day, yet had no sun or moon.

Genesis 1:9 "And God said, 'Let the waters under the heaven be gathered together unto one place, and let the dry land appear:' and it was so."

In many King James Bibles, you will notice before this Scripture a little flag. This is known as a pilcrow and helps determine where paragraphs begin. So, in a sense you get the best of both worlds with a KJV Bible: Verses, with the ability to read in paragraphs. If you want to outline a chapter, Book, or the entire Bible, this is a good place to start. I think pilcrows end in Hebrews, however. This is the fourth pilcrow of Genesis 1, so this is the beginning of the fourth paragraph in Genesis 1.

In verse 9, God speaks yet again. And when God speaks, things happen. "And it was so" punctuates with authority God's power in speaking. The waters are here gathered into one place, and the dry land appears. Evidently the land was not apparent before this. And

God gathered the water into specified areas. This will be enumerated further in verse 10.

Genesis 1:10 "And God called the dry land Earth; and the gathering together of the waters called the Seas: and God saw that it was good."

The Seas would be the equivalent to what we evidently call Oceans. But this was before the dramatic upheaval during the coming Flood of Genesis 7-9. God was here preparing for organic life upon Earth. And the eventual hydraulic cycle. We need to keep in mind that the Antediluvian world was possibly far different than the post-flood world. Many young earth scientists believe that the mountains were smaller before the Flood of Noah. And many of the names of pre-flood locations were brought over by Noah's family to the other side of the flood, yet they would not have been congruent to the pre-flood locations, necessarily.

Some see here in this verse one large body of water that was called the plural Seas. This may be so, but not necessitated. Even if it was one large body of water, possibly trenches beneath the sea level separated them into various quadrants. And the Earth could have been in a Pangea-like state at this time as well, but again, not necessarily.

Questions arise. Where did Rivers come from? We find four in Chapter 2. Were there more created here? Lakes and Ponds? Was there rain during this time, or even before the Flood at all (No seems to be the answer, but there is some dispute. If there was no rain, did the Hydraulic Cycle not begin until after the Flood? There could have been some type of rotation between Rivers and the Seas, but that induces questions again of salt and fresh water. Also, if there was evaporation, how did lakes and ponds if they existed, get replenished?)? Were the Seas then salt water? Whence did salt and fresh water originate? Did it have something to do with the Flood? Verse 10 does not seem like the place that gives answers on these points. As we continue reading, we may come back to some if not all these questions. What we do know is that God saw that it was good. This is the 2nd mention in Genesis of God's creation being good.

Genesis 1:11 "And God said, 'Let the earth bring forth grass, the herb yielding seed, and the fruit tree yielding fruit after his kind, whose seed is in itself, upon the earth:' and it was so."

Verse 9 seems to have begun the third day of creation, Tuesday October 25th, according to Ussher. Before this time, spiritual beings had been created (at least that is the majority view. Some feel that the stars created on day four refer to angels), matter, light, but no organic or biological life. Molecules and atoms, yes. Elements, yes. But no life in the material realm. But now life comes. And man does not come first. Neither does the animal kingdom. But rather vegetation. Most YEC (Young Earth Creationists) would say living microbiological organisms were created on their respective days. And that verse 16, among others around it concerning the astronomical heavens, would preclude other organic life in the Universe besides on Planet Earth.

This is the fourth instance of the phrase "God said" in chapter 1. Four times before this verse we find God "called," or named things. Again, there is great power in God's Word. When God speaks, people should listen. And the "God called" phrase is interesting. If the law of 1st Mention is followed (and I do not think it is an absolute law as I have previously stated), then in the New Testament the term "called" would indicate "named." This appears to be the case in at least some instances (James 2:7 for example) and may be useful in other interpretive contexts as well.

The Earth here brings forth grass, herbs that yield seed, and fruit trees. So, the earth brought them forth, God did not plant them whole in the ground, creating them beforehand. This seems to be significant for a couple of reasons. First, if the seed is a type of the Word as stated in Mark 4 and Matthew 13, that is how the Word of God works. It is planted in the ground of our hearts, and then brings forth fruit. Secondly, we will see how this aligns with or differs from the creation of other things in Genesis 1 and 2. Also, those who would say the days here are longer than 24-hour days, would say under normal germination processes, this process would have taken months, or in some cases, years. But we need to remember we were not under normal processes yet. The sun and moon are not created until the next day.

We are here introduced to the Law of Biogenesis. Life produces life. Abiogenesis and spontaneous generation are refuted theories. I recall Pasteur's beaker being used to debunk this theory in the 19th century. Annie Wood Besant and others of the Theosophical Society put spells on him because they realized this was a fatal blow to Evolutionary Theory. So, God, who is Life, produces life. The life is in the seed. Within the seed is the potential to fill the earth with the product of the seed. Amazing complexity is in the genetic structure of the seed. Can someone tell me how that could have evolved? So, God had plants to grow from the earth. Then each product was created with seeds for self-replication. We also see in this verse the law of kinds (genus, species, families, and the like). Genetic walls are built into the seed which ensures that which was is encoded in the cell is what is produced. Change comes from within DNA, not from without. Cut off a 1,000 generations of rat tails, and the rodent DNA still says rats will reproduce with tails. Haeckelian acquired characteristics is considered fairy tale science. The law of kinds, DNA, and genetic walls does not allow for evolution. This is observable science.

How could the complexity of DNA in a seed evolve? Science has no answers. God does. Genesis 1:11 is the only possible answer to the conundrum. Could the pine tree exist without the "seed"? How would it get to the next generation of pine trees? But how did the first pine tree get here without a seed? And how could a seed evolve? What chain of processes preceded it? As you can see, Genesis is the only possible solution, beside alien spermantation and such like, which is absurd, and only serves to kick the can down the road. Reputable Scientists like Hoyle, Wickramsinghe, and even Dawkins either advocate the idea, or at least consider it. Many other Scientists do as well. The problems confronted by the evolutionary conundrum are thought to be solved by circumstances inherent in an alien civilization, which may have different scientific laws than we have. Trans-dimensionality and such nonsense. I thought science was to be observable and repeatable. The lengths people go to avoid God, is much more absurd than the Bible narrative itself. At least what Scripture purports corresponds to reality.

Genesis 1:12 "And the earth brought forth grass, and herb yielding seed after his kind, and the tree yielding fruit, whose seed was in itself, after his kind: and God saw that it was good."

What God said, happened. This is still true today. We see plant life springs from the earth with the ability to reproduce within itself. A type of the Gospel to us. We are born of the Word and can share new life with others. And God here sees it was good. Now some would speculate that it was superfluous for God to see that it was good. Since He is all-knowing, wouldn't He know it is good without having to look? This may speak more to God's sense of beauty, complexity, and propriety. He knew it would be good. But He saw it as well. This does not necessitate Openness Theology, where God does not know the future. Openness is a radical expression of man's free will. God knows the possibilities, and the outcomes of the possibilities, but He does not know for sure which possibility mankind will choose according to Openness. So, God's mind, in this scenario, is like multiplied spider webs. Every second, a bird could fly up, down, perch, get a worm, etc. And God knows each millisecond of possibilities, and the ones that follow. But each living creature has freewill. In some permutations of the doctrine it is just Man that has this ability to freely choose. But if God is truly Omniscient, all knowing, He knows what one will choose all the time, from eternity past, into eternity future. But God's foreknowledge is not causative. Just because He knows, that does not destroy our free will. If we quit choosing, we have still made a choice, and He knew it all along. But He did not cause it.

Some would wonder when was microscopic life created (getting back to that)? Living, small organisms. I am not sure. You could make the argument here that the life-giving soil had to have the microorganisms in it at this juncture. But that is not so, since there is life here before photosynthesis and the ecological cycle of oxygen/carbon dioxide. You could also make the case for Days five and six, and possibly even day four. As I mentioned before, the consensus view is that it was on its own day of creation. So, a water-based organism would be created on day five and so on. But a soil-based organism? Day one? Day three? Day six?

Genesis 1:13 "And the evening and the morning were the third day."

Again, notice Biblically, and hence to the Jews the day begins in the evening, or more specifically to the Jews, at 6 p.m. Jesus rose from the dead on the third day. Life springs from the earth on the third day of creation. Typology, perhaps?

Genesis 1:14 "And God said, 'Let there be lights in the firmament of the heaven to divide the day from the night; and let them be for signs, and for seasons, and for days, and years:'"

Here the astronomical objects are created by the Word of God. A Psalm would be in order. Psalm 8:3 "When I consider thy heavens, the work of thy fingers, the moon and the stars, which thou hast ordained;" Just as in Genesis 1:1, 2, it appears that God spoke it, then fashioned these celestial objects, in this case with His fingers. I can imagine David looking at the sky, without light pollution, knowing there is a God. I used to lay on the small hillside beside my home as a teenager and tell God, I did not care what anyone said, I knew He was there. Nature tends to draw us to God. In America, rural residents have a much higher belief in God than urban dwellers. In rural settings, you are surrounded by unspoiled creation in every direction. In urban settings we are surrounded by manmade buildings and streets, and other sinful humans. Even the sky is shrouded by light at night. So, the thoughts about our Creator are sometimes more distant. But there is great revival in cities, nonetheless.

    The Creative act that is occurring here is that celestial objects are being placed in the second heaven. They are placed there for a reason. They are for signs, seasons, days, and years. Some would say since days would now be predicated on these celestial objects, that the first three days may have been of an indeterminate length of time, and the 23-hour 56 minute+ days began at day four. All I can say to that is that you would have plant life here for a long time, serving no real purpose. I see no need for that, except an attempt to fit the Bible in a modern scientific milieu.

Another discussion among creation scientists is that the years before the Flood were shorter than after the Flood. Not much shorter, but 360 days. The paper I read on it seemed to have real merit. But I am not learned enough in that area to offer a proper rendering of its validity. All I can say is, possibly. It had something to do with the friction rates of the reconstituted surface of the earth, and more so with the current tilt of the earth's axis. The theory is that the tilt was non-existent or less extant before the Flood, and this is where our extra few days currently come from in a year, 360 to the current 365+ days.

Celestial objects would also be for signs. The phenomenon of eclipses is fascinating. They show the exacting precision of rotational shadows, and the size of the objects during the eclipse. It is as if it were meticulously designed for eclipses to be observed on earth, or it is one of the most monumental coincidences that one could conceive. I choose the former.

Abraham was to look at the stars. Joshua commanded the sun to stand still. A star was seen at Jesus' birth. Darkness was over the world at His death. Darkness hung for three days in Egypt. The stars in their courses fought against Sisera. Orion, Arcturus, Pleiades, and the Mazzaroth are all mentioned in Scripture, and God calls the stars by their names according to Psalm 147:4. Stars fall from heaven in Revelation. The sun scorches men there as well. Hezekiah's sundial went 10 degrees backward. There will be no need of the sun anymore in eternity future. The sun turns to blackness, and the moon to blood before the coming of the day of the Lord. Signs.

But not just signs, but also seasons. Some have wondered whether there were seasons before the Flood. Others would say things would have been idyllic before the Fall. But since it probably did not rain before the Flood, and things were perfect in paradise, does this mean there were no seasons? The theory mentioned earlier (I think from

Bill Cooper, but it could be UK Creation Science Movement or Walt Brown, or even ICR) about the earth not having a tilt, or not much of one before the Flood enters the discussion here. The Noahic Covenant contains seasons in Genesis 8:22. If this were prophesying seasons to begin after the Flood, or did they begin after the Fall, or whether they began immediately, would be a matter of much discussion. And we must be careful not to ask foolish and unlearned questions, because they gender strifes (2 Timothy 2:23). I think it is ok to ask the question, just do not build a doctrine there, possibly. However, it happened, I think God designed seasons from the outset. There was a cool of the day in Eden, so possibly God could have seasons, but not as pronounced, before the Flood and even before the Fall. These less pronounced seasons would explain the mega-fauna and fossils at the poles. And the plants still only partially digested in the belly of frozen mammoths in the frozen tundra of Siberia. The poles were not always frozen, it seems.

The celestial bodies were for days, as well. This leads to an interesting discussion, namely, if the days were current days in length before the creation of the sun that would mean that the sun and moon cycle were superimposed upon an already existing system, and are not causative, per se. The sun and moon appear to have been placed in an already existing time framework. And when the sun and moon are no more in the end of the Book of Revelation, there is still the Tree of Life producing fruit each month. A time system. So, it appears that our current length of day, or at least the one pre-Flood, is something both anterior and posterior to the solar day. Interesting.

Another consideration is if the days before day 4 were not really 24-hour days, but very long days, possibly millions or billions of years in length, the lunar tide system would not have been functioning. And this would have a dramatic effect on earth. It has been said the earth could not exist without the moon. But it did for at least 3 days.

Among other considerations are the 24-hour day itself. Some think that the days before the Flood were exactly 24-hours in length. But because of the earth tilt that occurred during the Flood, the lunar drag effect has caused the loss of 3+ minutes every day, elongating the year as discussed earlier.

In verse 3 Light was created. Here lights are created in a material fashion. The sun, the moon, the stars, the nebulae, quasars, galaxies, and the like. But there is still a division of light and darkness. This seems to be a Biblical type of holiness. Holiness means "separation." Light and dark are forever separate. We are in the world, but not of it. The Sun gives light. The moon has no light, it merely reflects light.

The sun is a type of Jesus Christ, the Sun of Righteousness with healing in His wings (penumbra). And the moon is possibly to be typified as us. The only light we have comes from Jesus. We have none in ourselves. But we can reflect His glory. And there is a dark side in us, like the moon, that never sees light. Our sinful nature. Some have said the moon also typifies satan who comes as an angel of light and is also darkness, yet with no power of himself. Little wonder that the word "lunacy" comes from "lunar." And the fact that the moon approximates the Pacific basin, well, I have no opinion on the possible implications if any of that, other than the fact that I think the moon was created by God, and not taken from the earth.

So, everything in the Universe was created around the Earth? Yes. Does this indicate geocentrism? No, but rather the Anthropic Principle, which states that everything is created with Earth, and us, in mind. Most models of geocentrism would indicate the sun revolves around the earth, and not vice versa. I do believe Copernicus got it right. He would not allow his writings to be published until after his death in 1543. He did not want to suffer the fate of Galileo several decades later, or an even worse fate. But the Earth came before the sun, moon, and the stars, and even the Universe itself (the firmament or expanse). This is what Scripture teaches. Now if by geocentrism one means that the earth was created first, and everything else afterwards, then yes, the Bible does teach that.

Another fascinating study that it would be remiss if I at least did not mention it, is the study of ancient calendars. Sumerian, Babylonian, Akkadian, Egyptian, and Aztec are incredible studies. They tend to validate Scripture. Bill Cooper of the Creation Science Movement has been my source for these scintillating Scriptural studies. As an aside, the current Hebrew months are named from the Babylonian.

Genesis 1:15 "And let them be for lights in the firmament of the heaven to give light upon the earth: and it was so."

So, all these lights, the sun, moon, and stars, are in the firmament of the heaven (2nd heaven) and give light upon the earth. It is fascinating in the extreme that many of these lights for earth would not be accessible until the time Near Earth Platforms were developed, like the Hubble telescope, for example. God is extravagant. He made plants in the lowest oceans we are just discovering. He causes flowers to bloom in uninhabited deserts. He created the world of the micro that we are just uncovering. And the expansive astronomical heavens exploding in beauty and intensity. It was estimated in Abraham's day he could see around 7,000 stars with the naked eye. Today we know they are in the 100's of trillions, and we haven't found the edge of the Universe yet. Yet they are for earth. Earth evidently sat in empty space for a few days until God created astronomy on the 4th day.

Again, we see the emphatic power of God. "And it was so," the Scripture declares. Part of omnipotence demands an unstop-ability. 1 Corinthians 15 is also interesting to study at this point. As is Revelation 20-22. It seems that quite possibly in eternity future the Universe will in a sense return to the day three state. Yes, there will be a new heaven and a new earth. But it seems that during that time, with the New Jerusalem hovering majestically above the earth, glistening, with God's glory reflecting in the foundation stones possibly, the earth will be once again alone in the "material" Universe. Or maybe not. Of the increase of His government there shall be no end. Discussion could go on for quite some time here.

When was the New Jerusalem created? Genesis 1:1 or anterior? Is New Jerusalem the same as Jerusalem which is above? Heaven in Genesis 1? What questions! We do know according to Psalm 113:6 that even Heaven cannot contain the infinite God. C.S. Lewis in Perelandra has one of the most fascinating discourses that continues for several pages between the Watchers. Speaking of which, who are they, and when were they created? More wonderful discussion of Holy Writ. Beautiful discussion, of eternal things. Not football or politics, but things that are eternal.

Genesis 1:16 "And God made two great lights; the greater light to rule the day, and the lesser light to rule the night: he made the stars also."

Everything here seems based on the Anthropic Model. More specifically, since man was not yet created, it was based on earth at this time. Earth is created. The Foundation Stone for creation is claimed to be in Jerusalem (Jewish tradition, and possibly Muslim). Then space is created, the expanse or firmament. So, earth was in existence before space according to Genesis 1. Then things are created to fill up the vastness of space. If Heaven is God's Throne, and earth is His footstool according to Isaiah 66:1, possibly this is it how it began in Genesis 1:1, God's Throne, and footstool. Then space (firmament) separated God's Throne from His footstool (Earth). So, the earth originally rested upon nothing, not even space. Possibly it was God's footstool, because it was where satan was cast after his expulsion from Heaven. And he is under God's feet as indicated in Romans 16:24, and Genesis 3:15. We are seated in heavenly places as stated in Ephesians 2. This might help to shine more light on the Church's position in all of this.

So, the two great lights are from the perspective of earth, not generally in space. Space obviously makes the sun and moon relatively diminutive. God is highly concerned about things on earth, more so than other celestial objects, no matter how beautiful. It has been said many ancients from non-biblical societies thought that the moon was larger than the sun. It is fascinating to examine what ancient civilizations knew about the stars, and the solar and lunar cycles. They knew the progressions of some stars 25,000 years into the future in at least a few cases. Thales of Miletus correctly predicted a solar eclipse on May 28, 585 BC. There are entire tomes written about the astronomical observations and calculations of the ancients. Ancient man was not dumb. His cranial capacity was enormous even after the Flood, according to statues and drawings we have. Adam had been perfect and lived in perfection. We are slowly deteriorating. We no longer live to be near 1,000 years old. Again, the phrase found here "to rule" is solely from the perspective of Earth.

The phrase "he made the stars also" is one of the most stunning short series of words ever written. All are one syllable. Five words, to be exact. The longest is five letters. Eighteen letters in total. And in these five short words, it is recorded that God made the trillion upon trillions of stars, and all the celestial heavens. And He did this almost as an afterthought, "also." It has been rightly noted by Willmington that God wrote fifty chapters on the tabernacle, and five words on the stars. It shows where God's priorities are. I would also assume that the planets of our solar system were created here as well. Much has been made on starlight. Creation is supposedly disproved because it would take millions and in some cases billions of years for starlight to reach us, yet we can see the stars. So, the earth and stars must be old, it is said. Some thoughts on this. Evidence shows that the speed of light is not a constant but is decreasing. This is an inconvenient fact for science, who would rather it be a constant. So, possibly the speed of light was much faster before the Fall, and then in the world that followed. Or, since everything was made with Earth as its starting point, maybe God created the stars from here and placed them in the sky, with their initial light trailing from here to their final place in the sky. Or, perhaps God made the starlight move supernaturally fast, since the stars are for the purpose and pleasure of man. DeYoung does a masterful job showing scientifically that there is no contradiction of starlight with a young Earth. And if starlight was really travelling to earth, we should be seeing new stars on a regular basis appear in the night sky, as various starlights complete their journey to Earth. But this is not happening.

Lunar recession is a great proof of a young Earth, as is the symbiotic relation of the moon and Earth. The moon is receding from the Earth about two inches per year. If the earth were much over 6,000 years of age, the lunar gravitation which currently causes our beneficial tides, would wreak havoc and destruction on planet earth. And before that it would have just crashed into the earth. So, if current processes extend backwards just a few millennia, they would be an impossibility. The same is true for the sun. It is decreasing in size at the rate of 5 feet per second. Just a few thousand years ago, the earth would be unbearably hot from the closeness of the sun, and life on earth would be impossible. These are a few of the many reasons for the young earth postulate.

The earth was here before the sun. One of the speculations of how the earth and the other planets, moons, and asteroids developed into our solar system is that the sun gradually flung off material over time as it rotated, and these became planets once they cooled sufficiently. Or possibly other solids were trapped in the sun's gravitational pull. This of course is ridiculous in the extreme. Gas never becomes a solid, much less with the mantle, core, water, soil, etc. you find on planet earth. It is difficult to believe this ridiculous idea was the explanation in some scientific circles of why the earth's core was hot. No, Earth came first, then the sun and the moon according to Scripture.

Genesis 1:17 "And God set them in the firmament of the heaven to give light upon the earth,"

God made them and set them. Everything is designed for us. God set the stars, moons, and other celestial objects exactly where they needed to be. And He called them by their names (Psalm 147:4 "He telleth the number of the stars; he calleth them all by their names."). That is the reason Seiss and Bullinger among many others thought that there was some ancient significance to the names of the stars and constellation. Virgo the virgin, Scorpio, Gemini, Leo, etc. Reading works on this subject is fascinating. God named them and placed them, and it seems many ancient civilizations had some recognition of their importance. The names are relatively congruent in many older cultures. And certainly I, looking at the night sky, would never dream of forming the stars into constellations. They look like independent entities to me. But there they are. Now this cannot be mentioned in today's Church society much. It strikes of astrology. Most of today's conservative Biblicists would say that what God named the stars and constellations is known only to Him, and the rest is paganism. The Jews had their Mazzaroth, and it was known in Job's time. God mentions it in Job 38:22 where He says, "Canst thou bring forth Mazzaroth in his season? or canst thou guide Arcturus with his sons?" Mazzaroth is the twelve signs of the zodiac and their related thirty-six constellations. So, God knew of these 48-star configurations, and tells Job He did it. Interesting! Study it, just do not go into astrology. That is paganism.

Another wonder that fascinates astronomers is the fact that the stars in the night sky are perfectly attuned for us to see and examine, but they are not too bright. If the Milky Way, for example was just a little brighter, we would have 24-hours of light. Stars appear, but they are just points of light in the darkness. And they are still there during the day. There is just a superimposing light, the Sun that outshines them all so you cannot even see them. I can see the typology there.

Genesis 1:18 "And to rule over the day and over the night, and to divide the light from the darkness: and God saw that it was good."

So, the Sun rules the day, and the moon rules the night. There are always stars in the sky. But you cannot see the other stars because of the brightness of the Sun. "But unto you that fear my name shall the Sun of righteousness arise with healing in his wings; and ye shall go forth, and grow up as calves of the stall." Malachi 4:2. It is easy to see the typology. The Sun represents God, and His glory excels every other star in brightness.

We go back to the verse 4 principle. Light and darkness are to be divided. This is holiness. "Qadosh" in Hebrew and "hagio" in Greek mean holiness and have as a root "separation." We are in the world but not of the world. Jesus was a friend of sinners, but He did not sin. We are not isolationists or live in compounds away from the maddening crowd. But the Spirit of God and the Name of Jesus make us different from the world at large. We are new creatures, a different kind.

The Sun does not cease to exist just because we cannot see it. God is still in control of our lives even in the darkest of nights. This is yet another thought of how God constructed the world.

God sees the astronomical heavens as good. Matter is not evil as the docetists and gnostics taught. God said it was good. But it is never to be worshipped or exalted, only God is worthy of that. Creation bows to the Creator.

This is the fourth mention of the word "good" in Genesis 1.

Genesis 1:19 "And the evening and the morning were the fourth day."

So, all the celestial objects were completed on the fourth day. This is Amazing, and far more impressive than any Big Bang, and its accidental confluences over billions of years. Even man's fallen imagination cannot replicate the reality of everything in the astronomical heavens occurring in 1 day.

Genesis 1:20 "And God said, 'Let the waters bring forth abundantly the moving creature that hath life, and fowl that may fly above the earth in the open firmament of heaven.'"

Fish and fowl are here created on the fifth day, out of water. Not soil, not ex nihilo, but out of water. I find it immensely fascinating that fish and fowl were created before land animals. Whales, sharks, catfish, bass, jellyfish, eels, sea horses, manatees, along with eagles, hawks, sparrows, and bluebirds. Instantaneously, by the Word of God. And they were brought forth in abundance. The moving creature that hath life in verse 20 refers to the aquatic kingdom.

"Firmament" means the first heavens in this context that is within the earth's atmosphere. Flat earth proponents would say that the firmament here is the same as the astronomical firmament in verses 6-8. Hence in their viewpoint, the birds would be flying in the same sphere as the stars, moon, and sun, just a little lower down. But the text does say, "open firmament of heaven," so that would seem to preclude a conflation of the atmospheric and astronomical heavens. The Catholic Church never really taught flat earth, though they did teach geo-centrism. And God did create earth first, and everything extended outward from that up to the Spiritual Heaven. But everything does not revolve around the earth. It seems that John Draper in 1874 presented two rather obscure theologians from antiquity that seemed to teach a flat earth, and then conflated that with all of Christendom. And the lie was born from there. Like Columbus having difficulty finding a crew because of the prevalent belief in a flat earth. This evidently did not happen. It is a fraud of history perpetuated in the popular mind.

Much is made of man's body having compounds of the dust of the earth in it. I have never studied whether fish and fowl have large propensities of water in their bodies due to their original creation. It would be an intriguing study, but mere speculation on my part at this point.

Going back to flat-earthism. YouTube has made the impossible possible, so to speak. Well-presented error can deceive many. And almost anything can garner a following. Samuel Clemens said a lie can go around the world before the truth can get his shoes on.

Genesis 1:21 "And God created great whales, and every living creature that moveth, which the waters brought forth abundantly, after their kind, and every winged fowl after his kind: and God saw that it was good."

Great whales are specifically singled out by God. Not leviathan, not giant squids, but large (great) whales. Whales of course would play a role in the typology of the resurrection. Jonah was swallowed by a whale, and Jesus likened that to His resurrection. Notice the term "every" in reference to fish and winged fowl. This totally precludes evolution from one species to another. Also notice the fixation of species as mentioned by the word "kind." This again says there were various genus and species created, and they would be relatively immutable. And this is exactly what the fossil record shows. Fossils from whatever strata they are found show the same things that are alive today. There are no transitional fossils in the fossil record, and certainly not the chains of fossils from one kind to another, that evolution and Darwin say should be there, and should be the vast majority of the fossil record.

"Kinds" are exactly what we see in DNA and the laws of genetics. There is a fixity of each species, and only slight variations are possible within the genetic walls of each kind.

If the Bible were not inspired, how would Moses know of great whales, since he lived in Egypt? The Bible is full of these type questions that further strengthen the case for the Divine Inspiration of the Holy Scriptures. And God once again sees His creation as good. Hence, man, who is in the image of God, has a fascination for it as well. And just as God created the stars in five words, all the amazing underwater fish are likewise created with no effort by our all-powerful God. Creation lets us stand in awe of God.

Also, when it says every living creature that moveth, some may speculate that this refers to the living creatures in the angelic realm found in Revelation. It does not appear to me that it does, but rather earthbound terrestrial beings, whether fish or fowl.

Genesis 1:22 "And God blessed them, saying, 'Be fruitful, and multiply, and fill the waters in the seas, and let fowl multiply in the earth.'"

Here we have the first recorded use of the word "blessed." God speaks blessing here. And He spoke this blessing to fowls and fish. So, God created them abundantly, with all the various species, and possibly a good amount of each species, not just the singular male and female of the Adam and Eve model. Then He blesses them to reproduce. The reproductive systems of all living creatures could not have evolved. Evolution for these processes is impossible because they only work within fully operating systems. Partial systems would not be passed down from generation to generation, because they would not be beneficial. And of course, there would not be a "generation," because procreation would not be occurring. It seems to me an intractable problem for evolution, of many. Now, if I were defending evolution, I would propose various mechanisms where these things could occur. I may quote authorities on the subject. I may bring ridicule on the creationist side. But the problems would still be there. The subject would just become clouded. A good argument is not necessarily true, sometimes it just clouds the truth. Well-presented error is still error.

This is the first Biblical usage of the word "blessed," or any derivative thereof, as mentioned above. With blessing comes increase as seen here. The subject of "blessing" figures prominently in Genesis. The Patriarchs took the subject of blessing very seriously. Jacob was willing to deceive for it. Isaac was sure it would occur. Even in Jesus' day, people wanted Jesus to lay hands on their children for blessing. Notice blessing entailed speaking here.

God wanted the air and waters filled with life. In this blessed pre-sin world seen here, overcrowding did not seem to be an issue.

Ezekiel 1:10 presents an interesting discussion concerning living creatures. It reads, "As for the likeness of their faces, they four had the face of a man, and the face of a lion, on the right side: and they four had the face of an ox on the left side; they four also had the face of an eagle." These are the "living creatures," which seem to be congruent with Cherubim's (but that is another discussion entirely.). The "living creatures" were evidently formed before the fifth day of creation (Job 38:7). Bear with me here. God created them with eagle, man, ox, and lion faces, which would mean these archetypes existed in heaven before they were on earth. Existing for an indeterminate amount of time on the living creatures' faces. Or else God gave the living creatures these faces after He created the eagle, man, ox, and lion on earth. So, did these angelic beings come first, or the animal kingdom of earth? I would go with the former consideration. But it is incredibly interesting to think about. And if cherubs with their 4 faces came first, this would mean that each of these animals had an archetype, at least in the face, in heaven.

With the command to fill the seas, it would indicate that the aquatic kingdom was limited in distribution and number. But yet the seed was in them, blessed by God, with the capacity to fill the Universe if conditions were right. One male and female pair of whales had the potential within them to fill millions of Oceans with whales. That is a fascinating consideration.

Some say the command to be fruitful and multiply has been abrogated, either by the Fall, or by practical concerns that earth is overcrowded. Thomas Malthus seems to have used some variation of this argument. I do not see Biblically where the command to be fruitful and multiply has ever been rescinded. But in the Church age, maybe soul winning is part of the equation (see 1 Corinthians 7 to explore this further). Of the increase of His government there shall be no end.

Genesis 1:23 "And the evening and the morning were the fifth day."

Fowl and fish are created. Migratory instincts were instilled. The understanding and blessing to be fruitful and multiply is given. And 24-hour days are necessitated. If the fish and the fowl were multiplying for thousands of years in a perfect pre-fall world, the earth would have been quickly over-crowded. No death to cull the herd, so to speak. This would have been Thursday October 27th, 4004 BC according to Ussher's excellent chronological system.

Genesis 1:24 "And God said, 'Let the earth bring forth the living creature after his kind, cattle, and creeping thing, and beast of the earth after his kind: and it was so.'"

"And God said" is repeated for the seventh time in Genesis 1. The earth now brings forth as the waters did in day five. The first five days have been absolutely, amazing, from light, to plants, to astronomy, and all fish and fowl. Day six is not less enthralling. We continue to notice when God speaks, creation happens.

There are either four classes created here, or one class with three sub-species. It could be living creature is the genus, or overarching class. And cattle, creeping thing, and beast of the earth are the sub-species.

Cattle would refer to domesticated animals. Creeping thing would consist of beavers, ferrets, caterpillars, roaches, mice, and the like. Possibly even bacteria and flagellum. They were created sometime in the first six days unless they are the result of the Fall. Beast of the earth would be things like lions, tigers, Cape buffalo, rhino's, and dinosaurs, among many other things.

Let us get a reminder of who is doing the creating here. John 1:3 says, "All things were made by him; and without him was not anything made that was made." 1:10 reads, "He was in the world, and the world was made by him, and the world knew him not." This is speaking of Jesus, of course.

"Kind" once again refers to species, and the genetic specificity in each DNA strand. This is found throughout the fossil record and continues to this day. This is a remarkable observation in the Text, and a strong attestation to the truthfulness of the Biblical record.

Genesis 1:25 "And God made the beast of the earth after his kind, and cattle after their kind, and every thing that creepeth upon the earth after his kind: and God saw that it was good."

Notice "made" and "create" are here synonymous. They are used interchangeably. Other things to take note of are:

1) "Kind" as a genetic wall is again emphasized 3 times in this verse.
2) The descriptive "every thing" is here reserved for creeping things. This possibly indicates that there were more creeping things than the other two genres.
3) God, once again, for the 6th time, describes creation as good. Matter is not evil. Our sinful nature, satan, and his kingdom are evil.
4) This entire verse rules out gradual evolution and "hopeful monsters" of Stephen Jay Gould's Punctuated Equilibrium Theory.

Genesis 1:26 "And God said, 'Let us make man in our image, after our likeness: and let them have dominion over the fish of the sea, and over the fowl of the air, and over the cattle, and over all the earth, and over every creeping thing that creepeth upon the earth.'"

This is the longest verse in chapter 1 with 50 words, and in some ways the most discussed. 3 times in this verse God refers to the act of making man in a plural form. Now the most natural explanation to this is that God was referring to Cherubim's, or other angels. The traditional Jewish explanation has been angels, who appear as men throughout Scripture, except for Zechariah 5:9 (seemingly evil spirits there). Three good reasons for thinking these are Cherubim's God is referring to are:

1) Ezekiel 1:5 "Also out of the midst thereof came the likeness of four living creatures. And this was their appearance; they had the likeness of a man." As discussed earlier, the living creatures appear to be another name for cherubim. And they had the likeness of a man. Notice even the same term is used to describe them, "likeness." See verse 10 of Ezekiel 1 also.
2) Ezekiel 1:8 reads, "And they had the hands of a man under their wings on their four sides; and they four had their faces and their wings." So along with a general likeness, and a face of a man, they also had hands as a man.
3) Also, the next place a plural is used in reference to God speaking is in Genesis 3:22, 24 and the context seems clear He is there referring to Cherubim's. 3:22: "And the LORD God said, Behold, the man is become as one of us, to know good and evil: and now, lest he put forth his hand, and take also of the tree of life, and eat, and live for ever:" Notice the word "us." 3:24 reads, "So he drove out the man; and he placed at the east of the garden of Eden Cherubim's, and a flaming sword which turned every way, to keep the way of the tree of life." So again here, it strongly seems that God was referring to the Cherubim's, who are said to be in the likeness of a man, and who were created before mankind. Adam Clarke, I think takes this view of Genesis 3. The reference for the living creatures being Cherubim's is Ezekiel 10:15, which reads "And the cherubim were lifted up. This is the living creature that I saw by the river of Chebar."

The pushback on this is that only God is the Creator. And whoever God is referring to seems to be participating in the act of creation. Now in Revelation 4:6, 7, these "living creatures" are seen (four beasts with the same description of the Cherubim's) in the midst of the Throne of God. So that is something to consider. The Hebrew word for God here is "Elohim." Angels are referred to by the same Hebrew word in Psalm 8:5.

Since Elohim is seen as a plural of majesty, possibly God was speaking to Himself. The Royalty of England, and other countries throughout history, have referred to themselves in the plural. Even in the Koran Allah speaks of himself in the plural quite often. And people in general talk to themselves in the plural also. "Let's" is a common contraction which can be used in the singular and is short for "let us."

Since God dwells outside of time, as well as in time, He could have been referring to the man Christ Jesus here, as the Lamb slain from the foundation of the world. Since all things were made by Jesus, predicated upon Him, this is entirely possible and plausible. Or He could have been referring to the Word, the visible of the invisible God, but not a separate Person.

Monotheism rejects multipolarities in a pantheon of gods. The "us" and "our" definitely, do not echo original polytheism as some assert. This is not coming from Babylon, Sumer, or Akkad. This is written at God's direction by a One God Hebrew, Moses.

If three Persons were here referred to, then either tritheism must be true, or three Adams must have been created. Since neither one of those postulates is true, this verse must be interpreted in a Monotheistic way.

Gene Edwards in his Divine Romance book offers another fascinating look at the creation of Adam. He speculates that Adam was originally a spirit since God is a Spirit. And a spirit only. That flesh and blood was the result of the Fall. Fascinating, but I do not think I would teach that as doctrine.

Man was never meant to be alone. Even in this verse, man is referred to as "them," indicating there were more to come. According to verse 27, He was referring to Adam and Eve as man, as in mankind. Chapter 2, speaking of the creation of man and woman, happened on the 6th day. Some have tried to say that the "man" created in Genesis 1 were not Adam and Eve. I do not see that.

Since man was created in the image of God, he was created to rule. He was God's highest creation. He has the ethical attributes of God as holiness. And if hell is in the center of the earth, and earth is satan's prison house, not only is satan under God's feet on God's footstool, a being in God's image was sent to take over the outer part of the prison house.

Man was created to rule. As a free moral agent with free will, he was created to have fellowship with God. We read much about "kind" in Genesis 1. God was creating something in His image and likeness, His "kind," to eventually be His bride and family.

Genesis 1:27 "So God created man in his own image, in the image of God created he him; male and female created he them."

Many people say man was created to take satan's place. I use man in the Biblical sense here, to refer to mankind in general. If satan was a musical instrument according to Ezekiel 28, then we are as well. If satan as a cherub was in the image of a man, we of course, are as well. I am not sure how true this replacement theology is. I do find similarities in original purpose, however. But not totally, unless of course satan was created to originally rule over the pre Genesis 1 creation that was destroyed by the so-called satanic flood, which is where some try to get billions of years for the Earth's age, and dinosaurs, etc. I have earlier pronounced my disbelief in this theory.

Another interesting question I got from a student at Indiana Bible College was, is Eve in the image of God? It certainly seems she was. The language of verses 26 and 27 give extremely strong indication of this. But I guess the reasoning goes, if the image of God is the future Man Christ Jesus, then Eve could not be in the image of God. I would guess this means "human being," though. That seems the most logical interpretation. Of course, there are those that interpret Scripture of when we see Him, we shall be like Him, to mean all will be 33-year old males in heaven. I think that is overly literal. And I am a Biblical literalist.

It is true that Adam and Eve are not named here in Chapter 1. This is what gives rise to the thought that the Genesis 1 creation is different than the Genesis 2 creation as far as man goes. There were two different creations of man according to this theory. Again, when we get to Genesis 2, we will treat it as if they are the same account, one from a generalized viewpoint, and the other giving the specifics. But this only deals with man. There was a further creation in chapter 2, but not of man, unless you count Eve coming out of

Adam's side. It is also wise to take note that Adam is called the first man in 1 Corinthians 15:45, 47. Those Passages should end the matter.

It is noticeable that now God creates man in His image, clearly singular. So, God was not speaking to a God Committee in verse 26. I have a YouTube video of nine different explanations of verses 26 and 27. I think I have found another explanation since then, at least a possibility.

Genesis 1:28 "And God blessed them, and God said unto them, 'Be fruitful, and multiply, and replenish the earth, and subdue it: and have dominion over the fish of the sea, and over the fowl of the air, and over every living thing that moveth upon the earth.'"

So, God blessed the yet unnamed Adam and Eve. So, the first thing God does is bless Adam and Eve. Then He commands them. Much is to be unpacked here. Noah curses Canaan. So, it seems that verbal blessing and cursing were a powerful thing not just with God, but with man the image of God. Since man was (is) in the image of God that part of God's nature seems to have been passed down to us. Words matter. Words are powerful.

Look at the progression mentioned in verse 28. Blessing, then fruitfulness, multiplication, replenishing, subduing, and dominion. It almost sounds like a new convert's course. We are blessed with the new birth, we bear fruit, we multiply (win souls), and then begin to win at spiritual warfare.

Much has been made about the word "replenish." For something to be replenished, it had to be plenished (filled) before, or so goes the reasoning. This word, possibly more than any other argument, is the cause of the pre-Adamite theory. As I studied this word, especially in its 1611 context, it merely means "to fill." It has no connotations of previous existence necessary or implied, whether in English or Hebrew.

God speaks here to unfallen mankind. We were created to respond to His Word. And we are to be fruitful and multiply. Birth control has only been readily available since the mid-20th century. Catholics officially do not believe in Birth control pills and methods. Evangelicals by and large do. Conception seems to be the dividing line.

Subduing the earth entails to "dress" and to "keep" it. It does not mean to disregard and mistreat. Without virtue signaling or giving a hat tip to the radical earth firsters, there is a balance. God had the land lie fallow every seven years in Israel. God did not have Adam strip mine Eden. Being a good steward over God's resources is a very Biblical concept. To dress and keep the garden was a command in Genesis 2:15. Did this include pruning? I wonder. There is a ditch on both sides of the road between good stewardship and an over emphasis on the earth and the things in it. But mankind is to have dominion over it.

Mankind is here given dominion over every animal as well. Now before the Fall, there was no suffering and death, so dominion must have included organization. It also included naming the animals, as we see in Chapter 2. After the Fall, this dominion would continue, but I am not sure this would include driving species to extinction. This would not be good stewardship. We are informed in the fossil record that 80% of all things found therein are now extinct. I would assume we are to continue to be good stewards of the animals, especially if the animal kingdom were to be fruitful and multiply also.

Genesis 1:29 "And God said, 'Behold, I have given you every herb bearing seed, which is upon the face of all the earth, and every tree, in the which is the fruit of a tree yielding seed; to you it shall be for meat.'"

God continues here to speak to man. In verses 28-30 He speaks approximately 111 words to Adam and Eve. "You" here is plural, so God is speaking to both Adam and Eve. Since man was originally a vegetarian, some say this is the perfect diet still. While it is healthy, we do live in fallen bodies. I have read some studies which suggest a totally plant based diet is not optimally healthy, and that at least some meat is required. Many Vegan social media influencers have gone off vegan lifestyles because it was hurtful to their bodies.

Here, God gave. Everything He did in Creation was a giving, loving act. And He gave every herb and fruit for food. Fascinating. Now, were plants in the sea given for our food, as well? If earth here means the "globe" or "sphere," then yes. If it merely means "dry land," then possibly still, yes. Silence does not indicate a negative, many times. Silence means it is not recorded, but not that it did not occur. Be that as it may, it seems in this context that terra firma is referred to here and not under the Seas. Could Adam swim? Could he get things from the four Rivers of Chapter 2, or the Seas? Did he name the fish also? Could the fish walk on land? Questions, questions, and so few answers. But we have answers to everything we need for life and godliness.

When God created plant life on Day three of Creation, it was with man in mind, primarily. Of course, animals ate it as well. But it is clear, that with man in God's image, after His likeness, and with dominion, man was His ultimate priority. Not just vegetation was primarily for mankind, however. The stars and the astronomical realm seem to be for man's purview as well, at least significantly. Could Adam see the farthest reaches of the Universe before the Fall? Could he possibly go back and forth to Heaven? Did he assemble with the sons of God, as in Job 1 and 2? We will know when we see Jesus, and then we will know even as we are now known.

Did hornets sting before the Fall? Wasps, bees, mosquitoes, scorpions, and their ilk? I would say no. But if they did sting, it was harmless and painless in this halcyonic world. Were roaches and spiders pests? No. Did these things become so after the Fall? Yes. Did a hornet have a sting before the Fall? I have no idea.

Genesis 1:30 "And to every beast of the earth, and to every fowl of the air, and to every thing that creepeth upon the earth, wherein there is life, I have given every green herb for meat: and it was so."

So, animals were originally vegetarian. Notice, the beasts of the earth and the fowl, and the creeping things got green herbs here. Did the fangs on beasts grow at the Fall, or were they already there? Were the digestive systems pre-setup to digest meats? I just do not know, but I would assume so.

Notice the beautiful word "life." Animals have life. Possibly far more so before the Fall.

Another interesting word is "green." Chlorophyll, aligning so close molecularly with human blood, was a created sign of vibrant plant life.

So, lions, tigers, leopards, hyenas, and all we would call carnivores or omnivores, were originally vegetarian. It seems in this state the lion and the lamb truly did have the ability to dwell together in peace. And that day will come again.

Genesis 1:31 "And God saw every thing that he had made, and, behold, it was very good. And the evening and the morning were the sixth day."

While still in the sixth day, God saw everything that He had made in that day and previously, and it was very good. Individually it was good. Cumulatively, it was very good. Think for a moment what is recorded in Genesis chapter 1. Light is created. Heaven, with its celestial splendor. Earth, and water are made. Thousands of types of plants and trees. The stars, galaxies, and nebulae pulsating in a stellar display. The planets with Saturn's rings, Jupiter's storm, and Mars crimson red. The constellations. Our own yellow Sun perfectly positioned for life on earth. Our satellite the Moon, again formed with meticulous precision. The atmosphere, molecules, and atoms. Complex bacteria finely tuned. And then each animal, fish, and bird, with their designed characteristics, their beauty, and intricacies of creation, whether skeletal structure, skin, fur, nerves, brains, blood, motor skills, aerodynamic capabilities in the case of birds, fins and scales for fish, and so on. All, in six short days. And more than I can describe. The blueness of the sky, the scent of the plant, the radiance of the sunrise and sunset, the redness of the rose, and exploding variation of it all. The deep spectrum of color. Paradise indeed.

In verse 31, a magisterial view of creation is given. God seeing that it was very good reinforces the fact that creation itself is not evil. Matter is not evil as the Gnostics and Manichean's would have us believe. Even in its fallen state, David wondered in awe at creation (Psalm

8 and 139, for example). Paul said it was groaning and travailing waiting for our manifestation. Revelation 4:11 shares that creation is solely for God's glory. It says, "Thou art worthy, O Lord, to receive glory and honour and power: for thou hast created all things, and for thy pleasure they are and were created."

In verse 31 "made" is seen as synonymous with "create." And the sixth day is here completed. A large part of chapter 2 is just a retelling of parts of chapter 1, and especially the sixth day of creation, with more specifics given.

Doing a deep dive into Genesis 1, I am convinced that six, 24-hour days are here intended to be communicated. The ages or epochs of times that some postulate may sound reasonable on the surface. But the more you study it, the more you see the vast problems that arise with such an interpretation. Psalm 90:4, also penned by Moses, says "For a thousand years in thy sight are but as yesterday when it is past, and as a watch in the night." The day/1,000-year theory must take into account that it is also considered a 3 or 4-hour period for a thousand years as well, a watch in the night. It is hyperbole. 2 Peter 3:8 says "But, beloved, be not ignorant of this one thing, that one day is with the Lord as a thousand years, and a thousand years as one day." The key word in this verse is "as." It does not say it is, but again, it is like 1,000 years. The most similarity I can see between the day/thousand-year paradigm is possibly since the millennium is 1,000 years of Jesus' rule, maybe this present age will last 6,000 years with the last 1,000 representing the Sabbath. But this has nothing to do with the 24-hour days of Genesis 1. Exodus 20:11 really seems to seal it, when it reads, "For in six days the LORD made heaven and earth, the sea, and all that in them is, and rested the seventh day: wherefore the LORD blessed the sabbath day, and hallowed it." Symbiosis, the reliance of things upon other things, seals it scientifically, among a host of other proofs.

Chapter 2

As we shall see, it seems that the second chapter of Genesis after verse 3 is just a retelling in the specifics of the sixth day of creation. This will become apparent as we progress through the chapter. Some have attempted to differentiate between the creation accounts. There have been those that postulated two classes of humans created, those in 1:26 and 27, and those in Chapter 2. Others have tried to discredit the entire Creation Narrative by saying there are contradictions between the accounts of chapters 1 and 2. Neither of these positions is seen to be true by the evidence.

Genesis 2:1 "Thus the heavens and the earth were finished, and all the host of them."

Now "heavens" is in the plural here in 2:1, because the atmospheric and astronomical heavens are added to the third heaven that God created in Genesis 1:1. All of creation was finished, both organic and inorganic. It is not evolving. It is not Theistic Evolution. It is not progressive creationism, but rather finished. The potential for all things living was locked in the seed. Looking at Hebrews 7:9, we see the viability of the seed. It reads, "And as I may so say, Levi also, who receiveth tithes, payed tithes in Abraham." So, the seed that would eventually become Levi was in Abraham his great-grandfather. The seed in Abraham was recognized as Levi himself. This Scripture is also to be considered when discussing birth control and Onan.

Genesis 2:2 "And on the seventh day God ended his work which he had made; and he rested on the seventh day from all his work which he had made."

Paul, or whoever the earthly writer of Hebrews was (I believe it was Paul), refers to this verse, and has an interesting, inspired interpretation of it. In Hebrews 4:3, 4 it says, "For we which have believed do enter into rest, as he said, As I have sworn in my wrath, if they shall enter into my rest: although the works were finished from the foundation of the world." "For he spake in a certain place of the seventh day on this wise, And God did rest the seventh day from all his works." I have heard of a Pastor preach on Kingdom praying. That God has already answered every prayer in the first 6 days of creation, it is just up to us to pray it into existence. Maybe this is where Revelation 13:8b comes in, when it says "…the Lamb slain from the foundation of the world." I know everything is done in the mind of God. Other interpretations more esoteric than this are beyond me.

We once again see "made" being synonymous with "create." In Gen. 1:1, 21, 27 speaking of this process, God uses the word "created" 5 times. He also uses it in 2:3 and 4. But He also uses the term "make" or "made" in 1:7, 16, 25, 26, 31, 2:2-4. In 2:3, 4 He even uses "created" and "made" in the same verses. So, they are often synonymous.

Resting is not something the infinite, all powerful God needs to do. It simply means He stopped. God never gets tired and never needs to rest. And we must remember the Sabbath was made for man, and not man for the Sabbath. It is for man, not God. It is emblematic. Also, unlike tithing and unclean versus clean animals, we see no hint of the Sabbath among men until Moses' time, and it is specifically mentioned as being for Israel.

Some would possibly interpret verse 2 as pointing toward Deism. God set the world in motion, and now it just performs. No, God is still actively involved in His creation. He knows when sparrows fall to the ground, among a vast number of other things. And He is intimately involved with His creation. He is not only the Watchmaker of Paley, but He is also the active Participant of Creation. But He is not the Ghost in the machine, per se. This would tend toward Spinozian pantheism.

Genesis 2:3 "And God blessed the seventh day, and sanctified it: because that in it he had rested from all his work which God created and made."

The seventh day, Saturday, has a special blessing attached to it, and is sanctified (set apart). Now for Sabbatarians this would be conclusive. The Sabbath is for all. It has a special blessing attached to it. And this verse in isolation could be seen as conclusive. But as I look for evidence of this being applied to the Church or Gentiles in the remainder of Scripture, I find the evidence wanting. In Acts 15, the Gentiles were not commanded to keep the Sabbath. Colossians 2 and Romans 14 specifically says not to judge someone on Sabbath adherence. A key question to be considered however, is this; is the Sabbath still in effect for Jewish Christians and not for Gentile Christians? Again, it was not mentioned in the Acts 15 protocols. And it is mentioned by Jesus in Matthew 24:20, which reads, "But pray ye that your flight be not in the winter, neither on the sabbath day:" Many interpret this passage as being specifically to Jews. I hope I have an open mind and objectivity, and a willingness to change my position on this. Since rest is associated with the Holy Ghost (Isaiah 28:12), most people I know interpret the fulfillment of the Sabbath in our day with the Holy Ghost rest. Once again notice in this verse the congruent nature of "created" and "made." There is no difference here. But each context of these two words must be taken individually. Just because they are synonymous here does not mean they are consistently synonymous, necessarily.

Genesis 2:4 "These are the generations of the heavens and of the earth when they were created, in the day that the LORD God made the earth and the heavens,"

This is the first of 18 uses of the word "generations" in Genesis. The phrase "These are the generations" is used 10 times in Genesis, and the phrase "the book of generations" once. Many look on this phrase "the beginnings" as scrolls or books that Moses used as source material. I see no reason to think that is the case. Others see this as a natural way to divide Genesis for study. I think that is perfectly fine.

Notice "heavens" is plural, consistent with the other two heavens created after Genesis 1:1. The Jews also think of the heavens as a first, second, and third type proposition. Paul brings this up in 2 Corinthians 12:2.

"Generations" is a word normally used for organic or living substances. But here it is used for material creation in a general sense. "Day" is used in verse 4 as a period of time here meaning six, 24-hour days. Since Hebrew and Greek have a paucity of words when compared to English, a few thousand words instead of around a million, the same word must be used for multiple situations oftentimes. There is no mention of "evening and morning" with this usage, so it indicates it is different than the Chapter 1 usage. Deer or deer, sheep or sheep, context interprets its numerical equivalent. So it is here with the word, "day." So, day is here used for six days. The so called "law of first reference" says that however a word is used first in Scripture that is how it is to be used or has significance in that way throughout all of Scripture. The use of "day" here, as opposed to 24-hour days in Chapter 1, shows us that the law of first reference is not an absolute law of Biblical interpretation. I am not sure it is necessarily significant at all - in that I am not sure it is even a general rule of thumb. I think that it was probably promulgated by certain groups (the Seventh Day Adventists have traditionally used it quite a bit), to help promote a certain doctrine or doctrines.

Also, again we see "created" and "made" are synonymous. This is the first usage in Scripture of the term "LORD God" or Jehovah Elohim. That is significant. It is used 11 times in Chapter 2, and nine more times in Chapter 3. It is then not used again until after the Flood, in Genesis 9:26. Jehovah Elohim is often called the covenant name of God. Exodus 6:3 says, "And I appeared unto Abraham, unto Isaac, and unto Jacob, by the name of God Almighty, but by my name JEHOVAH was I not known to them." Of course, Jehovah was used often throughout the time-period of the Patriarchs. This merely means they did not fully understand the full Nature and implications of that Name. El Shaddai (Almighty God) was primarily how He was known to the Patriarchs. Also, the name Jehovah does not seem to have been isolated to Biblical usage. My archaeology Professor mentioned they had found Jehovah used six different times throughout the ANE (Ancient Near East), if memory serves me correctly. Paleo- Hebrew seems to be the language Moses would have been writing in. David H. Benner has written masterful tomes on this phenomenon of the literature of Mosaic inspiration. Douglas Petrovich has good archaeological evidence that Paleo-Hebrew was the first consonantal alphabet, and was developed by Joseph, Ephraim, and Manasseh in Egypt. Please study his conclusions for yourself, for they are fascinating. Our earliest Hebrew writings, from Hezekiah's tunnel to the Numbers 6:24-26 silver scrolls are all in Paleo-Hebrew.

Genesis 2:5 "And every plant of the field before it was in the earth, and every herb of the field before it grew: for the LORD God had not caused it to rain upon the earth, and there was not a man to till the ground."

So, God created the plants and the herbs, then planted them. What came first, the seed or the plant? Why, the plant, as is seen here. And what came first the chicken or the egg? The chicken. The Bible contains the answer! But in verse 9 we see that the plants in Eden were from the ground, and then grew.

There are no transitional plant forms in the fossil record. All appear fully formed. How many have become extinct over the years, I have no idea. But God created them all, and then planted them, in all their wondrous variety. Could you imagine what that panoply of pre-Fall plants looked like in color, size, and shape? English, like Hebrew and Greek, is a picture language. It is meant to promote a picture in our thinking. It still does in non-electronic societies. One of the seeming unintended consequences of electronic media, it seems to stunt the painting of pictures in the theatre of the mind.

Jehovah Elohim causes rain. I use Jehovah because Riplinger has convinced me this is the original way, or closest to it in English, to pronounce the Tetragrammaton (Four Letters), LORD in the KJV.

Read her work, check her sources closely, before rejecting her work. I find it rather definitive. And Jehovah Elohim had not caused it to rain. Many, combining this with the next verse, think that it did not rain on earth until the Flood. That is quite possible. But the language does seem to imply that it takes rain to have plants grow in the earth, so possibly not. At the same time, from Moses' perspective 2,500 years or so later, you could say that it did not rain until Noah's Flood, and not do violence to Scripture.

And there was not a man to till the ground. This was obviously before Day six of Creation when Adam was made. The general context is describing Day three. So, it is a retelling of Day three from Chapter 1. And it describes one of man's tasks was to till the ground.

Genesis 2:6 "But there went up a mist from the earth, and watered the whole face of the ground."

This mist, many interpret as dew. But it was everywhere. How many of each plant did God create? Did He fill the face of the world with plant life? Or, as in the case with Adam and Eve, just enough for it to populate the earth gradually? If it was to be food for all of the animals, He must have planted multitudes of each kind, and filled quite a bit of the face of the earth with plant life, it would seem. And since plants are dependent upon CO_2 and we are dependent upon Oxygen, multitudes of animals were probably created as well for the plants to survive. So, this mist was everywhere, and there were no deserts in the early, perfect earth.

What caused the mist? God. Was it natural scientific laws of condensation, or something supernatural? Since God is the Creator, is there any real difference? What we call natural laws or scientific laws, are really processes created by God. I would say all qualifies as miraculous, whether it is from a law He instituted, or something He specially causes within His pre-instituted laws.

Genesis 2:7 "And the LORD God formed man of the dust of the ground, and breathed into his nostrils the breath of life; and man became a living soul."

Now we get into the specifics of how God created Adam, the first man. Man came of dust. Our vessels are vessels that began of clay. We received the breath of life. I find it fascinating that resuscitation can still be done upon the dead, on occasion, by us as the images of God blowing into the mouth and/or nose of one recently deceased.

And man became a living soul. The tripartite nature of man. Some Scriptures that are good to consider here are: Ecclesiastes 12:7 "Then shall the dust return to the earth as it was: and the spirit shall return unto God who gave it."

Genesis 3:19 "In the sweat of thy face shalt thou eat bread, till thou return unto the ground; for out of it wast thou taken: for dust thou art, and unto dust shalt thou return."

Psalm 104:29 "Thou hidest thy face, they are troubled: thou takest away their breath, they die, and return to their dust."

1 Thessalonians 5:23 "And the very God of peace sanctify you wholly; and I pray God your whole spirit and soul and body be preserved blameless unto the coming of our Lord Jesus Christ."

Some people are dichotomists. They see no difference between the soul and the spirit in man. I'm not sure how they reasonably interpret Hebrews 4:12 which reads, "For the word of God is quick, and powerful, and sharper than any two-edged sword, piercing even to the dividing asunder of soul and spirit, and of the joints and marrow, and is a discerner of the thoughts and intents of the heart." How can soul and spirit be divided if they are the same? Now it is true there is overlap in what soul and spirit represent, and how they are described in Scripture. Cartesian dualism, named after Rene Descarte's philosophy, says there is a "ghost' in the machine, so to speak. We are not the meat suit. We are not just the clay. There is a spiritual dimension to man. The Hobbian (Thomas Hobbes) organic development of the brain is to be rejected. We are more than nasty, short, brutish cells pieced together in our brain. We have a conscience, and an inbound knowledge of the Creator (Romans 1). Then our bodies die, the spiritual man will be somewhere for eternity.

Traditionally, the body, soul, and spirit are described as having the following functions. The body is the five senses. The soul is the mind, will, and emotions. The spirit in man is the conscience, communication, and intuition. But, of course, these are general designations, and there is overlap since we are 1 human being. At death, the body goes to the dust, the soul to either a place of bliss or torment, and the spirit returns to God who gave it. Luke 16 is also good to study in this regard.

Genesis 2:7 corresponds to 1:26-28, and is interesting to be read in conjunction with it. To reiterate, this is not a separate creation, but a retelling in the specifics of Genesis Chapter 1.

I have been pondering Creation versus evolution. Mankind had to be designed to digest plants and herbs. How could he have survived long eons of time while trying to develop this ability to eat and digest vegetation? And speaking of that, plants, animals, and man are dependent upon one another for breathing. They had to come in all at the same time, approximately.

God made man in His image according to Gen. 1:26, 27. Since this image included a physical body, this must have included the future incarnation of the last Adam, Jesus. Now God is a Spirit. And man has a spirit. God is the Word, and man has a soul. And man has a body, and God had a Body, in the man Christ Jesus. Since God dwells both outside and inside of time, no divine flesh is necessitated. Do divine flesh proponents think that God had a physical cell of zygote in heaven, awaiting to implant it in Mary? I am not sure.

So here is man, fearfully and wonderfully made. 90 foot tall as in Islam? The ability to travel between heaven and earth? Amazing in intricacies, complexities, and detail. Man was made as an adult. Fully formed like the plants were formed. Was he made 30 years of age in Bethlehem, as many speculate? The Scripture is silent.

Within Adam, just as in the herbs and plants, was the seed to fill all the world. We, in a sense, were contained in the bosom of Adam. Hebrews 7:9 is fascinating in this regard. When God created Adam, He created him with incredible potential.

Genesis 2:8 "And the LORD God planted a garden eastward in Eden; and there he put the man whom he had formed."

So, a territory named Eden, somewhere to the East of where Adam was formed, was the place God planted a garden. The Garden of Eden. And then God placed Adam in the garden He planted. All of this, through verse 25, happened on the sixth day, evidently.

Eden means "delights" or something synonymous. Some say "paradise." God is a good God. His intentions for man are clear. Pleasure, delight, fellowship with Him. God created man with good intentions. Peace and prosperity. Many Jews think Adam was created not at Bethlehem, but rather at Mount Moriah. And the rock in the mosque of Omar, besides being the place of Abraham's near sacrifice of Isaac, and the place the Ark of the Covenant rested on, was also the foundation stone for the world.

Genesis 2:9 "And out of the ground made the LORD God to grow every tree that is pleasant to the sight, and good for food; the tree of life also in the midst of the garden, and the tree of knowledge of good and evil.'

This is a special creation by God on the sixth day. This is not the third day creation of vegetation. But, yet, it had to within the first six days of creation, since God stopped creation on the sixth day. And the trees came out of the ground, not created then planted, as the herbs and plants were in verse 5. But notice only trees are mentioned here. It could be that trees were the exclusive purview of man, especially when you compare this with Genesis 1:29 and 30. I will re-post them here so you can see the specificity of language in this regard. 1:29 "And God said, 'Behold, I have given you every herb bearing seed, which is upon the face of all the earth, and every tree, in the which is the fruit of a tree yielding seed; to you it shall be for meat.'" This is written to man as is obvious from the context. Verse 30 "And to every beast of the earth, and to every fowl of the air, and to every thing that creepeth upon the earth, wherein there is life, I have given every green herb for meat: and it was so." So, it is interesting, the possible difference in diet of man and beast. But I am not sure it is significant. Maybe more on that later.

So every tree that was pleasant to the sight and good for food was given to Adam. This is the grace of God. And notice as well, two particular trees mentioned - the tree of life, and the tree of knowledge of good and evil. And look at their location, in the midst of the garden. The middle. So, wherever man went, the trees were there. And whenever Adam would go to partake of the tree of life, if he so needed to since there was no death, since there was no sin, the forbidden tree was right there. Possibly man would eat of the tree of life for pleasure and not necessity. Maybe it pointed to something else.

How big was the Garden of Eden? We do not know. We could guess, but it would be speculation at the end of the day. Were the trees in the midst of the garden, life and the knowledge of good and evil, significantly bigger than the other trees? What did they look like? It is unknown in this temporal realm.

If sin caused death, what was the significance of the tree of life? Symbolic or typological? The fruit on the tree of life in the New Testament era of grace is Jesus on the cross. He was crucified in a garden (John 19:41) and Gethsemane seems to have been a garden as well (John 18:1, 26; it means the "olive press." There are still olive trees there). What type of fruit was on the tree of life in Eden? Grapes, symbolic of His blood? Pomegranate? Unknown to us as far as I know. Jewish tradition says the knowledge of good and evil "fruit" was a loaf of bread. Some say it was figs, since Adam and Eve clothed themselves with fig leaves after the Fall. We encounter the tree of life again in the last chapter of Scripture. It is in the New Jerusalem. Revelation 22:2 reads, "In the midst of the street of it, and on either side of the river, was there the tree of life, which bare twelve manner of fruits, and yielded her fruit every month: and the leaves of the tree were for the healing of the nations." 22:14 says, "Blessed are they that do his commandments that they may have right to the tree of life, and may enter in through the gates into the city." And something at least very similar to the tree of life is mentioned in Ezekiel 47:12. And of course a tree healed the water at Marah. Where were these trees, of life and knowledge of good and evil, during the Flood? Were they destroyed with Eden? Or was Eden taken to the center of the earth and called paradise, where the thief on the cross went? Or was the tree of life miraculously taken up to the New Jerusalem before the

Flood? Interesting questions all. This is above all a thinking, prayerful commentary, by the way.

Man bears fruit when he is saved. The fruit of the Spirit. And it gives life to all who will eat of it. So, in some sense we have the tree of life within us as Christians.

Man was in a state of innocence. He had free will, yet the knowledge of good and evil was beyond him. This is not a symbolic parable, but actual events that show us how mankind has gotten to the place it currently has, and why the world is the way it is. Genesis is history, not allegory.

Man was to live in paradise in perpetuity. All was bliss, with fellowship with God, animals, Eve, and children. God stacked the deck heavily in man's favor. All was perfect, just avoid one tree. And it was there to show man had free moral agency. Man fell, but God is not to blame. God had set him up for success, and really could not have weighted the proceedings any more in man's favor, while maintaining freedom of the will. But God in His omniscience knew man would fall. And He had a plan in place for redemption.

Genesis 2:10 "And a river went out of Eden to water the garden; and from thence it was parted, and became into four heads."

So, there was more water in the early Earth than the seas and the mist. In this region called Eden one river gave birth to four. It also appears that the garden did not fill all of Eden, but was contained within Eden, with Eden being a region. Were other regions so named? And as we will see, the garden was an enclosed garden, with an entrance in the East, just like the Temple and the Tabernacle.

What kind of fish were there in these rivers? Is this the beginning of the fresh and salt-water division, or did that occur at the Flood? How beautiful the River that parted into four heads must have been. And the water itself, before sin, must have been absolutely exquisite. Was water necessary for man to live before the Fall? Or even food? Or was food just for pleasure? These are not foolish questions as mentioned in Scripture, but places the text naturally takes us to ponder and meditate upon it. And the answers are to be revealed in the resurrection. Just as angels eat manna, and can eat of earthly food, we would assume they ate only for pleasure and not provision.

Genesis 2:11 "The name of the first is Pison: that is it which compasseth the whole land of Havilah, where there is gold;"

Pison means "Increase" or "broad flowing." Three of the more popular guesses of what river it is referring to are the Ganges, Indus, and the Nile. Some also guesstimate the Araxes. The word "Pison" itself is a beautiful word picture of this life-giving stream. Havilah means "circle." Now Moses writes in the present tense. And he writes as if the river Pison still existed in his day. Or was he copying from a pre- Flood document that Noah brought through the Flood? So, I know the current school of thought is to say that these are different rivers than any that exist today because of the Deluge of Noah. But the language seems to indicate otherwise. Of course, if one believes this is a clay tablet that Noah carried on the ark, and that Moses used as a source, it makes sense for it to use the present tense being written before the Flood. But I find no Biblical evidence that Moses utilized sources like this.

Havilah is mentioned seven times in seven verses in the Bible. The location of Havilah has been variously seen as Sheba, Arabia, Yemen, Turkey, Ethiopia, Afghanistan, and India, among other places. But there was gold there. So, God created the earth with gold upon it. New Jerusalem is made entirely of pure gold, so it is no surprise that God made gold on earth. It is speculated that all the gold on Earth would fit into an Olympic size swimming pool. So, the New Jerusalem is magnified in splendor to scale.

Genesis 2:12 "And the gold of that land is good: there is bdellium and the onyx stone."

Again, the present tense is used. Bdellium, is most commonly referred to as an aromatic resin that has various purposes and is used as an essential oil.

Genesis 2:13 "And the name of the second river is Gihon: the same is it that compasseth the whole land of Ethiopia."

Of course, the most obvious river that would compass the whole land of Ethiopia would be the Nile, or the Abay River which is called the Blue Nile. Many other postulations have been proffered, but it is important to consider topographical changes that may have occurred in this area due to the Flood and/ or the dividing of the earth in the time of Peleg. The five other references to Gihon in Scripture refer to a spring around Jerusalem. If Gihon means something different here than in the other five places it is used in Scripture, the law of first reference would be further invalidated. The term Gihon means to "gush" or "spring forth."

Genesis 2:14 "And the name of the third river is Hiddekel: that is it which goeth toward the east of Assyria. And the fourth river is Euphrates."

The reason some feel there are interpolations in the Torah, and really the rest of the Old Testament, is because they would argue that Assyria, for example would have been unknown at Creation. But, the land of Eden was named before Adam was created, so why not Assyria? And if this is Moses writing what it was called in his day, the need for positing interpolations ceases, and the Mosaic authorship of the Pentateuch is preserved.

Hiddekel means "rapid," and is the current Tigris River, which now extends for 1,150 miles. The land between the Tigris and the Euphrates form the Fertile Crescent, and the land between them is also known as Mesopotamia (the land between the rivers). This has long been seen as part of the man's earliest history, and many call it the cradle of civilization.

The Euphrates River is currently approximately 1,700 miles long. Its name means "I announce" or "I declare." It is one of the most famous rivers in the world, along with the Yangtze, Indus, Nile, Amazon, and Mississippi Rivers.

So, the Garden of delights would have been well watered, with fresh, life-giving, uncorrupted, pure water. And it is quite possible that God named these rivers, just as He did Eden. The term Eden is used 20 times in Scripture, including 14 times from 2 Kings onward. There seems to have been multiple people named Eden.

Genesis 2:15 "And the LORD God took the man, and put him into the garden of Eden to dress it and to keep it."

Jehovah Elohim takes man from the west and puts him into the Garden of Eden to dress it and keep it. Man was created with purpose. Order was one of Adam's original tasks, just as God brought order out of chaos in the beginning. Plants and trees grow, so possibly pruning and hedging was even in that ideal state required. Keeping the garden would have been to keep up with it. Some people say the word, "keep" has a connotation of to guard. That would be interesting, as we see later the garden had one entrance, on the east, and possibly the serpent was not supposed to be in there. That would indicate that Adam was somehow derelict in his duty to keep the garden. This may be extrapolating too much from what was intended from Scripture, however.

This is the sixth of 11 times LORD God (Jehovah Elohim) is used in Chapter 2. This is the first time, and one of three times in Genesis 2 and 3, that the Garden is called the Garden of Eden.

I want to go back to the purpose of Adam in the garden. Work had a delight aspect to it. God worked for six days. Man is in the image of God, so man works as well. Man had a purpose. Maybe Adam was to plant and harvest crops. Keep the grass mowed. Were there weeds? Surely not, but probably something existed that became weeds after the Fall. Mist was needed, so even though there was no death as of yet it seems things were needed to ensure maximum fruitfulness at least.

It seems that men are constantly trying to recreate Eden. Not just Nebuchadnezzar's Hanging Gardens, but utopian fantasies abound. The grace of God is needed for viable, peaceful, prosperous governments upon earth. It is as if man knows intrinsically our current state is not what was originally intended. Echoes of Eden abound all around us. Adam was to work, but in perfection, and never grow tired. This all changed with the curse.

When we dress, as Adam did the Garden, it is more than covering, as we see here. There is to be an orderliness and arrangement to it.

Genesis 2:16 "And the LORD God commanded the man, saying, Of every tree of the garden thou mayest freely eat:"

Let us progress through this verse. The LORD God commanded man. Not the animals, but man. So, God began issuing commandments In the Garden. It did not begin at Sinai with the Decalogue (Ten Commandments). God is our Superior, so in His love and wisdom, He commands us. But His commandments are not grievous, but for our benefit. When the Word is preached, we can either choose to obey it or not. Preachers are to speak as the oracles of God (1 Peter 4:11) and are to preach the word (2 Timothy 4:2). Faith cometh by hearing, and hearing by the word of God. Man shall not live by bread alone, but by every word that proceedeth out of the mouth of God. Just as Adam was made in his very DNA to receive God's Word, so are we made to hear it as well. So, the Spirit gave man life, God's breath. And His Word told Him how to live.

Man could freely eat of every tree of the garden, save one. Eating would have been for enjoyment, and not for sustenance, it is assumed, as discussed earlier, since physical weakness and death came because of sin. Could Adam have overeaten? Did we even need nutrients and the like before the Fall? Did we sleep before the Fall on a regular basis? Or did Adam just look at the luminous stars, all being called by name, at night? Since God never sleeps, and Adam was in the unfallen state in the image of God...? Yet Jesus had no sinful nature, yet He slept. Did Adam have a belly button (one of the most asked Sunday school questions)? Adam was free to enjoy God's beauty and bounty. God stacked obedience in man's favor heavily. Man would be without excuse if he fell. And who could ever doubt the benevolent intentions of such a good God? Satan did, and got Eve to also. If we have eyes to see, God has still stacked everything in our favor. He draws us by His Spirit. He shed enough of His blood for all. He has poured out His Spirit on all flesh. He has 2 good angels for every 1 demon. If God be for us, who can be against us? It is not His will that any should perish, but that all should come to repentance and everlasting life.

Genesis 2:17 "But of the tree of the knowledge of good and evil, thou shalt not eat of it: for in the day that thou eatest thereof thou shalt surely die."

This is the second mention of this tree of the knowledge of good and evil mentioned in Scripture (2:9 was the first). Adam, being in the image of God, had knowledge. How much knowledge? Certainly not omniscient. Rather, in his innocent, holy, state, he knew only purity, and the knowledge associated with that. God desired to keep him in a state of beauty and holiness, free from the horrific damage of sin.

"The" tree indicates again there was only one tree, versus all the manifold blessings and wonder around Adam. Notice as well, it is not recorded here that Adam should not touch the tree or its fruit, only do not eat of it. Possibly this was an unwritten command. Possibly it was just obvious, that if he was not to eat of it, then he should not touch it, either. A few Scriptures are instructive here. The first is 1 Thessalonians 5:22, which reads, "Abstain from all appearance of evil." Genesis 3:3 says, "But of the fruit of the tree which is in the midst of the garden, God hath said, Ye shall not eat of it, neither shall ye touch it, lest ye die." Many have postulated that Adam added to the Word of God and gave Eve a non-Scriptural command. They usually are combating against Phariseeism when it is mentioned. But the first sin of mankind was not Adam lying or adding to God's Word. And it was not Eve lying. It was disobedience to God's Word, which equals rebellion. So, God must have spoken it either here to Adam and it is not recorded, or on another occasion, possibly to Adam and Eve together. Some say this is where the concept of the "fence around the law" comes from in Judaism. That we are not even to get close to evil. Some note also that Adam and Eve did not drop dead the same day they partook of the fruit. But since Adam died at 930 years of age, this could very well mean that since a day with the Lord equals a 1,000 years, and he died before the 1,000 years was up, this fulfilled this Word from God. Death, in its simplest definition, means "separation" from "life." Not that every time we say goodbye to someone death is involved. But our life. And Adam died spiritually, which is real life, in the day he ate. And notice "thou" (sing.) shall surely die. There was no way out. And since Eve and Adam were one flesh, Eve died also. Since Adam was the federal head of the planet, the entire animal world began the process of dying as well. The relationship between Genesis, and the theological concepts of the Book of Romans is worth exploring. Death came by sin. Life came by righteousness, the sinless One, Jesus Christ.

Was Adam the federal head of the Universe? If not, is the Universe decaying like earth? Or is it exempt from entropy? If the Universe is decaying, is it the result of satan's sin possibly? Or if sin entered into Earth, did it filter into the remainder of the Universe? Good questions all. The answer is worth a book all its own, I am sure.

Genesis 2:18 "And the LORD God said, 'It is not good that the man should be alone; I will make him an help meet for him.'"

Just as in Genesis 1, we here see God speaking. "God said" is used ten times in chap. 1. Here we have the LORD God saying. Ephesians 1:11 speaks thus, "In whom also we have obtained an inheritance, being predestinated according to the purpose of him who worketh all things after the counsel of his own will:" So God spoke. Angels heard it. It is also in His Word, the Holy Scriptures, so we hear it today.

Companionship, in order to be complete, had to be with like "kind." Since man was in the image of God, couldn't God have been perfect companionship with man? Wasn't this the point? Every other animal had male and female at this time. There was evidently some need for Adam to have companionship with another of like kind. Male and female. Was it for procreation only? Perhaps, but could God have made it where man procreated without Eve? Or is some reference to an eternal type seen here? The operative word in this passage is "alone." Somehow, even with fellowship among

God and animals, man would still be alone. And that is not good. So, fellowship is a Biblical principle we see from the very beginning.

God will make Adam an help that is meet for him. Good for him. From the beginning woman was created in a complementarian role. "He who findeth a wife findeth a good thing and obtaineth favor of the LORD." She was to be a help in dressing and keeping the garden and being perfectly compatible with Adam. "Help meet" is but 1 word in Hebrew. Again, as well, we see "make" being synonymous with "create."

Genesis 2:19 "And out of the ground the LORD God formed every beast of the field, and every fowl of the air; and brought them unto Adam to see what he would call them: and whatsoever Adam called every living creature, that was the name thereof.'

This is still the sixth day of creation. And this is a special creation by God to fill the Garden of Eden. Fowls were initially created the previous day, and seemingly out of water. Now God creates the beast of the field, formed as it is, and the fowl of the air, out of the ground. And He brings them to Adam, just as He would bring representatives to Noah 1,650 years or so later.

Now it says that God would see what He would call them. If God has all knowledge, didn't He know what Adam would call them? Or is some kind of radical Openness Theology required, or even radical free will? There is freedom of the will, for sure. But God can know and see at the same time. None of the erroneous Openness theology required.

And whatever Adam called every living creature, that was its name. God named things in Genesis 1:5, 8, and 10. Since Adam is in the image of God, and had dominion, he could name things also. And this verse is also the first time we find out the name of the man. "Adam" is first used in this verse and is found 31 times in 27 verses in the remainder of Scripture. Adam means "red," or "earth."

Going back to Adam naming, I think it is significant that at baptism, naming occurs. Just as a child was named at circumcision, we, like Adam, pronounce the name of Jesus upon someone at baptism.

And that becomes the family name. This was Adam exercising his dominion in the case of the animals. Another theme throughout the Pentateuch (the first five Books of the Bible), is the pronouncing of blessing. Just as God did in Chapter 1, Adam is pronouncing names in Chapter 2, but it may not have a blessing component with it. This goes forward into the New Testament, with prayers in the Name of Jesus, for healing and deliverance, authority and blessing.

When God formed these fowls and animals, possibly He made them westward where Adam was from, and brought them into Eden. Notice the silliness of making the 6 days of creation elongated periods of time. These animals were created then brought to Adam. They did not reproduce for thousands or millions of years. Scripture only allows for six, 24-hour day creationism.

What language was God speaking in Genesis? What language was Adam speaking? The assumption is that all the world spoke the same language until Babel in Genesis 11. Hebrew? Paleo-Hebrew? English, which is a derivative of Paleo-Hebrew and Greek? Sumerian, Akkadian, Egyptian, Babylonian, Chinese, or some lost and forgotten language? Most older theologians guess and surmise Hebrew in some form, or a cognate. Without delving too deeply into the debate, Hebrew does sound plausible to me, but there are other possibilities. An interesting Scripture in this regards in Zephaniah 3:9, which reads "For then will I turn to the people a pure language, that they may all call upon the name of the LORD, to serve him with one consent." If Joseph, Ephraim, and Manasseh really created the first consonantal language, as is now the current speculation of history and archeology, this would need to be investigated as well.

Genesis 2:20 "And Adam gave names to all cattle, and to the fowl of the air, and to every beast of the field; but for Adam there was not found an help meet for him."

Did Adam give names to creeping things as well? It is not mentioned that he did here. I would assume that he did however, since every beast of the field is put into the equation. Plants, trees, and herbs? Since he had dominion, quite possibly, but it is not recorded that he did. Bacteria and the micro-world? Possibly. Could Adam see the micro-world that requires intense magnification today? Maybe, but it also might blur the surrounding objects if he could. But he was perfect, in the image of God. How far into the Universe could Adam behold? Was there a vapor canopy that would inhibit long range viewing? Or could Adam even travel back and forth to the throne of God in heaven? These are all questions worth discussing and exploring. On the question of whether Adam in his unfallen state could travel to the throne of God, I have heard this is the reason that the blood had to be sprinkled on the heavenly mercy seat, as recorded in Hebrews. That Adam did not just start death and decay on earth, but the entire universe is decaying and running down, as we discussed previously. And maybe that is what we do in prayer, a poor imitation of what Adam used to be able to do at times. We go before the Throne of God, howbeit, not physically. But the Inhabitant of the Throne does live within the saved. Did Adam and God have daily communication in the Garden? That is supposition, and not explicitly stated in Scripture as far as I know. But it is taught oftentimes as doctrine.

The animal kingdom provided no help that was suitable for Adam. He needed a "like" companion. If we are to be the bride of Christ, that is why His Spirit in our lives is so important. We must be of God's kind. We take His name, and turn towards Him, and away from this fallen world. And His Spirit dwells within us. We become His family. Could Adam communicate with the animals? There are hints that he could. Who was he naming the animals for? Future humans and himself, of course. But quite possibly to speak with them as well. Eve did not seem startled that the serpent was speaking. Maybe it was the only animal that could, but why? Balaam's donkey shows us that God can have animals speak even now. The Fall probably diminished this capability, as it did so many other things. From perfection to the Fall. Yet animals with their various sounds and body language do seem to have non-language communication with humans still.

Did Adam name Dinosaurs? Yes. Fish? I would assume so. Were dinosaurs in the Garden? Yes, why not? From dinosaur legends such as Mkole Membe and the Loch Ness monster, to the Ica Stones (the real ones, not the frauds), to dinosaurs preserved with flesh and blood on them, human and dinosaur footprints together, and hundreds of dinosaur legends, of course man and dinosaurs were together, and there is no reason they would not have been in the Garden. Those that speculate otherwise are unfortunately ignorant of the evidence.

So, we see here it was not good for Adam to be alone. He needed companionship beside the animals. And that help was meet for him, other than God, of course. God possibly was still too "Almighty" for Adam, he needed something lower. We were made even a little lower than the angels.

Genesis 2:21 "And the LORD God caused a deep sleep to fall upon Adam, and he slept: and he took one of his ribs, and closed up the flesh instead thereof;"

The first surgery! Anesthesia and all. Did Adam sleep before the Fall? Maybe, but possibly it was just for recreation, like eating possibly was before the Fall, and not of necessity. So, God took one of Adam's ribs, and closed the flesh thereof instead. Blood comes from the marrow of the bone. So, Adam and Eve were one. This order of Divine creation is seen so powerfully in 1 Corinthians 11, 1 Timothy 2, and 1 Peter 3 among other places in Scripture.

When God took the rib out, it seems He took more than blood and bone out. Women think differently than men. They are separate but equal. Their emotions are in many cases different. Their functions are different. It is said in Scripture that Eve was for companionship and help. But surely reproduction must have been in mind as well unless Adam had some means of reproduction we do not know about today. But that is not the case. It was told to them to be fruitful and multiply. It took togetherness to reproduce.

So, 2:7-25 of Genesis was the sixth day of creation explained and examined in detail. Some say that Adam could not have named all the animals in one, 24-hour day. Name one every two seconds, and you have named 18,000 in ten hours. I think there was plenty of time. And of course, he was perfect. God was bringing them to him. Tiredness would not have been an issue.

This does happen to be the first mention of sleep in Scripture.

God rested the seventh day. Since man is in the image of God, man would quite possibly rest, but not sleep before the Fall, continuing our discussion from earlier. After the Fall, man would lose in a sense up to 1/3 of his life sleeping.

It is a misnomer that men have one less rib than women. Adam did, of course. But the fact that we do not actually disproves evolution. Acquired characteristics do not influence our DNA. Circumcision is not inherited from one generation to another. Amputees do not pass down that trait in their genes. So, the giraffe's long neck is not caused by gradual changes. Mendellian genetics disproves the theory of evolution that others have tried to foist upon the world. We know better. Science declares it. Acquired characteristics are considered a fairy tale now, except when it is needed to be dusted off to once again try and prove the collapsing theory of evolution.

Genesis 2:22 "And the rib, which the LORD God had taken from man, made he a woman, and brought her unto the man."

This seems to be a theme in the early part of Genesis. God creates Adam and brings him to the garden. God creates animals and brings them to Adam. Now God creates Eve and brings her to Adam. Now since God started with a rib, is "create" the proper term? He began with dust and made Adam, so I would say so. Again, it would appear that "made" and "create" are here once again synonymous. The Bible speaks of children being created, and they begin with a seed and an egg, so creation can have elements in place from the Creator.

God did not begin with dust in creating Eve, as with Adam. But He began with a rib from Adam. Could God have created Eve ex nihilo, out of nothing? Of course, He could have. But He chose to use material that He had formed from the dust in Adam. God made land animals from the earth in Chapter 1, and again fowls and land animals in 2:19 from the earth. But Eve came out of Adam, near His heart, so she would be dear to him. Blood and water came out of Jesus' side at Calvary, after His piercing, so the Church born of water and blood would be dear to Him as His bride. Typology seems to be very much intended.

As is often stated, Eve came not from Adam's foot that he should rule over her. And she was not from his head that she should rule over him. But rather she came from his side, as a help, so he could protect her. Matthew Henry has the classic look at this as far as I know. Being taken from near the lung, maybe that is why a woman can take a man's breath away. And being so close to his heart, maybe that is why a man will love a woman enough to die for her. She should share his heartbeat in help.

It seems marriage completes a man and a woman. Then they are finished, as the old joke goes. But really, in the ideal, it is for the procreation of children, and an incredible relationship. It takes 2 for procreation.

God bringing her to the man is representative of the first marriage in all probability. We are not sure of what, if any, things accompanied this bringing, except what is recorded in Scripture. It is unique, at least in the West that the bride still wants to remain hidden from the man until the ceremony.

Genesis 2:23 "And Adam said, This is now bone of my bones, and flesh of my flesh: she shall be called Woman, because she was taken out of Man."

Now we hear Adam speak for the first time. He had named the animals, but what he spoke is not recorded. The language he spoke in is not specified. Adam is referred to as a prophet in the New Testament (Luke 1:70). He speaks 46 words here in Genesis 2, and 38 more in Chapter 3, 39 if you count "Eve" in 3:20. So few words, so impactful for mankind. Some words uttered before the Fall, and some after. He spoke another word in 5:3. Adam spake of marriage and relationship before the Fall, and of shame and blame afterwards. We see him here calling her Woman, and in 3:20 Eve, and later naming a child Seth, just as he had named the animal kingdom.

Adam spoke in his pre-fallen state. "This is now bone of my bones" he says. What profoundness. And flesh of my flesh. She shall be called Woman, because she was taken out of the Man. Was Adam's flesh also used in the production of Eve? Or is this euphemistically speaking of the rib? That is a subject of much discussion. And of course, she was not yet called Eve. God called their name Adam (Gen. 5:2). They were so close in oneness, that they even had 1 name, but 2 biological designations (Man and Woman).

God could speak. Adam, made in God's image, could speak as well. Eve could also, as seen in Chapter 3. But of course, so could at least the serpent, and later a donkey.

Genesis 2:24 "Therefore shall a man leave his father and his mother, and shall cleave unto his wife: and they shall be one flesh."

Adam here begins to prophesy in His powerful, innocent state. Luke 1:70 says, "As he spake by the mouth of his holy prophets, which have been since the world began:" So prophets began with Adam, and began here, at least as the Scripture records.

Since God's command to Adam and the Woman were to be fruitful and multiply, Adam knew there would be other men and women in the world. And he knew that men would leave father and mother and begin new family units. He then saw that men would cleave unto their wives. Notice, first, the possessiveness. His wife. He would desire her. After the Fall, she would desire him. Not to say she did not before, but it is specifically mentioned there. He would hug her and hold her. Cleave to her, which I am sure had an emotional component as well.

And they shall be one flesh. The act of marriage. God meant it for procreation, but for pleasure as well. We have no idea of what it was like in a certain sense before the Fall. The gestation period and the like were surely less arduous. Adam and the Woman were the archetypical marriage, prepared for connubial bliss.

Was woman in the image of God? I remember being somewhat startled in a Bible class by that question from a student. He had a rather strong array of Scriptures suggesting she was not. Since I had never studied it, I had only assumed that she was, and I began to study the question in my journeys through Scripture. And I found she was. Years have passed, the proofs escape me, but she was. Their name was Adam. They were one flesh. She was in the image of God.

If Seth was in Adam's image, and he was in God's image, then the Woman coming from Adam would be as well.

So, Adam continues to speak on this sixth day of creation. Notice he speaks of "wife" in the singular, not in the plural. Monogamy was God's original creative intent. God created Adam and Eve, not Adam and a multiplicity of women.

Also, the question arises that if the man is to leave his father and mother, is the woman to do the same? Yes, of course. Look at the Scriptural examples. Rebekah, Rachel, Mary, Leah, Ruth, Esther, Rahab all left their families to begin a new one. David's wives did the same. I think it was unmentioned here because it was understood and assumed.

This is the first usage of the word "wife" in the Bible, among 397. In Hebrew, the word is "Ishshah," which means "woman," or the opposite of the man, or simply "wife." Women do seem to have a more difficult time leaving the family. Not in isolation, of course, but in God's plan of beginning their own family. Deuteronomy 24:5 gives a glimpse of this when it says, "When a man hath taken a new wife, he shall not go out to war, neither shall he be charged with any business: but he shall be free at home one year, and shall cheer up his wife which he hath taken." So, for 1 year it is just to be the husband and wife. And the husband's job is to cheer up his wife during that year. I wonder if that is where the concept of a honeymoon began?

I probably need to expound a little more on leaving mother and father. Of course, according to 1 Timothy 5, we are to provide for family on through struggling aunts. 1 Timothy 5:4 says, "But if any widow have children or nephews, let them learn first to shew piety at home, and to requite their parents: for that is good and acceptable before God." Notice the word "nephews." So, this would include aunts. But getting back to our mother-father household there comes a time that we cease obeying our parents, per se as we begin our own family unit, and rather honor them. Once we are on our own, in our own separate home and the like, the relationship shifts. We should always honor our parents, but that does not include obeying them in all cases. There are even instances that we do not obey even when we are under their tutelage, such as self- harm, breaking God's laws, and other narrow situations. For a marriage to be healthy, there needs to be privacy. You should not demean your spouse to your parents. Parents should not meddle in their grown children's affairs. These are just healthy relationships.

Genesis is a book of beginnings. This is how married life began. Original intent is seen, while in the next chapter we are introduced to the distortion of the Fall. What we see in Chapters 2 and 3 are normative, the pattern. What some would refer to as natural law.

Genesis 2:25 "And they were both naked, the man and his wife, and were not ashamed."

This is a profound statement. Naked and not ashamed. So, they were living in a state of pure innocence. This also indicates that after the Fall of man, people that were naked would be ashamed. Clothing and modest dress were introduced after the Fall of mankind. After the Fall is where the lust of the flesh, the lust of the eye, and the pride of life was introduced. That is called "the world" in 1 John 2:15-17. I do think it is interesting, though the word "world(s)" is used 292 times in Scripture, it doesn't appear until 1 Samuel 2:8. "Earth" is used before that.

"Naked" in some fashion is found 104 times in Scripture. "Nakedness" means to be uncovered, but it is not always used in reference to clothing. But here it does have that connotation, of being without clothing. So, clothing matters, as we will see further in Chapter 3. God is the Author of clothing. He wears it in Heaven and wore clothing as a Man upon Earth.

Could "naked" also have a fuller context here? Were Adam and the woman totally open books, so to speak, with their thoughts and intentions revealed and exposed? What we do know is there was no shame, no embarrassment. And clothing is not relegated to earth. God is clothed, angels appear clothed, seraphim in Isaiah 6 seem to have a sense of modesty. Possibly satan's fall made it where the angels were clothed? It really is just speculation, with no definitive answer this side of heaven to my knowledge.

Chapter 3

THINGS MOVE RAPIDLY IN THE FIRST two chapters of Genesis. While only six days are covered, everything that exists came into being in a sense. The rapidity of change continues into Chapter 3. Here we see the Fall of man. But it does not just effect man. The entire earth groans and travails to this day. And it possibly extended to the Universe, since Earth was created before the Universe, and the Universe was created "out" from the Earth, so to speak. The Earth was made subject unto vanity, but not willingly. Entropy sets in. The Second Law of Thermodynamics is enacted. Things are going from a more orderly state to a less orderly state. But it gets worse. That horrific enemy, death, with all its incumbent horrors, enters. And satan becomes the god of this world, instead of man having dominion. Eden's entrance is barred. The way to the tree of life is guarded by cherubim and a flaming sword turning every way. Hell expands herself. Fear and dread replace plenty and joy. All because of one act of disobedience. Later in Scripture we find that disobedience to God's commands are like rebellion and witchcraft. The human psyche remembers all of this. It constantly seeks for Eden, but usually in all the wrong places. It constantly seeks forbidden fruit. It wants a relationship with God, but on its terms, not God's. Chapter 3 could be seen as a fulcrum for the remainder of Scripture. Or it could be the beginning of a tale of sorrow and redemption, bookended by states of bliss under God's kingdom.

God did not destroy the tree of life. There was hope. It was guarded, but still there. A flaming sword guarded it. The Word of God is called a sword. It still guards the tree of life to this day. Fruit hanging from a tree gives life. Something else hanging on a tree would give life some 4,000 years later. Jesus. Eat of Him and live. A prophecy of hope is given even in the midst of despair. The woman, a virgin, would have a seed. It would defeat satan. It would bruise his head. But His heel must be bruised.

Here Paradise is lost. At the beginning of Chapter 3 all is bliss. By the end of Chapter 3, the seeds of every war, disease, famine, revenge, heinous crimes, brutal dictatorships, and the like are all implanted in the human species. Every despicable act is resident in the heart of man. Human nature loses the touch of the Divine and goes to the devilish. Plants die. Beauty is blighted. Animals become savage. Nature is now red and tooth and claw as Tennyson so aptly portrays it.

The ultimate disaster will lead to the ultimate triumph. The greater the defeat, the greater the victory. The Universe has been negatively affected. But the Creator of the Universe shows His love, and has a plan, already worked out in His foreknowledge, for Paradise to be restored. The Lamb was slain from the foundation of the world. Because of Jesus, there is hope. Without Jesus, you think it is bad now? Just wait. The ultimate disaster would have been if God would not have created everything by Jesus Christ.

Genesis 3:1 "Now the serpent was more subtil than any beast of the field which the LORD God had made. And he said unto the woman, Yea, hath God said, 'Ye shall not eat of every tree of the garden?'"

The serpent is here introduced. And the serpent is talking, and the woman is not frightened? Surely this must not have been an unusual event. How long were they in the garden before this took place? I have heard so many opinions. One thing we do know is that Adam was 130 when he begat Seth in Chapter 5. Before that, Cain and Abel had time to be born after the Fall, grow into men, and other unnamed children to be born and grow, and migrate. These are the known facts.

Many say Chapter 3 happened the day after Chapter 2. How do they know? Civilization must have been at least beginning, one would think for Adam and Eve to have the capacity to sew. Did they just invent that on the spot after the Fall? Maybe. But there is a distinct possibility that Adam and the Woman (she was not yet named Eve, but I will probably still call her Eve) obeyed God's Word to be fruitful and multiply. Would that offspring be the sons of God in Genesis 6? I do not know. But it seems possible, or at least something to consider. Is Adam and Eve, the Garden and the Fall, mythology, or symbolism? There is certainly nothing to indicate that it is. It is merely an attempt, those who think it is, to not upset modern sensibilities. Science has proven that Creation was not so, is the refrain. So, it must be referring to some higher truth. Or an embedded truth in the psyche of mankind. Jordan Peterson certainly presents it this way. It is very clear, however, that the writer is trying to communicate the historicity of the events, not a myth pointing towards higher truths.

Symbolism is not the main point here, but historical record.

The famous Temptation Seal of archeology depicts a man and a woman seated on either side of a tree loaded with fruit. Behind the woman is a standing serpent, at ear level with the woman. The man and the woman appear to have headdresses, possibly denoting kingship, and royalty. It certainly appears to be an echo of Eden, found in Sumer.

In 2:23, 24 Adam was either speaking to Eve, or just speaking into the air, to be recorded in Holy Writ. Here however, we have the subtil serpent speaking to Eve. Where was Adam? The later wording indicates he was right there. Adam's Father was God, and his mother the New Jerusalem possibly (Galatians 4:26; far too in detail to expound on here). Would Adam fulfill his own words, and leave Father and mother and cleave to his wife?

The serpent was evidently possessed by satan. The serpent, elsewhere called the tempter, was adding to the temptation of the tree. Temptation has a material and a spiritual component. Yet, we know God does not tempt anyone, nor can He be tempted. The tree was a test of obedience, not a temptation. But it became such.

The temptation was one of denial. God gave you every good thing, the world in perfect condition, but He has withholden this from you? Adam had dominion. He could name animals. All was perfect harmony. But satan wanted them to focus on the tiny, infinitesimal thing they could not have. We face the same thing today. We have eternal life, God within, prayer, power, the hope of eternal life. But satan wants us to focus on the rotting corpse of sin and the world's system. God's holiness forbids the destroying power of sin and disobedience, not the love, joy and peace that comes from God. The fruit of the Spirit is without law, which means it can be partaken of in limitless supply. Satan is the great inverter. What some call legalism, is really coming to God on His terms. Living as kingdom citizens. But of course, we must emphasize inward relationship as well. Freedom to sin is bondage. Liberty to walk in holiness is freedom, not the other way around.

Satan hides the consequences of sin. He hides the eternity in hell, the lake of fire, the loss of relationship with God, the pain, anguish, and heartbreak. He paints a veneer over sin. He tries, as here, to make God look bad. God won't give you that? God won't let you do what? God loves us so much, He doesn't want his children to partake of spiritual poison.

The serpent was a beast of the field, who evidently walked upright at this time, at least physically. "Yea, hath God said," is still a tactic of his today. He seeks to make people doubt God's Word. He also wants people to misinterpret Scripture, so they will get fleshly liberty which leads to spiritual bondage.

Then satan calls attention to God's prohibition, not His provision. Satan is truly subtil. And these "go to moves" of his we see in the Garden, we find that mankind, and even the Church, are still susceptible to them today.

Genesis 3:2 "And the woman said unto the serpent, We may eat of the fruit of the trees of the garden:"

Forty-four words were spoken by Eve in verses 2 and 3. Should she have spoken to the serpent? She had dominion over him according to 1:28. Should she, in this state of innocence, even have entertained for a moment the doubt that God loved her? That He is faithful, and abundantly giving in His Nature? Here, in verse 2, the woman appears to be defending God. She opens her defense with God's abundance. His provision.

Going back to the question of how long of an interval was between Chapters 2 and 3, there are some interesting things to consider. According to verse 16 of Chapter 3, it does seem that Eve was acquainted with childbearing. And in verse 8, it indicates they may have been in the Garden quite some time. But again, we really do not know for sure. Some contend that Chapter 3 is just an extension of Day Six.

When satan came to Jesus, Jesus quoted Scripture to him. The conversation between Eve and the devil is obviously not the way to win at spiritual warfare. We have weapons that are not carnal, but mighty through God to the pulling down of strongholds. Eve did as well. But she allowed doubt in God's love and provision to creep in. And then the beauty of the fruit kicked in. Doubt God, and make the world look enticing. These are still tactics satan uses today. People worship and serve the creature more than the Creator. James 1:14-16 says, "But every man is tempted, when he is drawn away of his own lust, and enticed." "Then when lust hath conceived, it bringeth forth sin: and sin, when it is finished, bringeth forth death." "Do not err, my beloved brethren." We see this paradigm from James quite nicely here in Genesis 3, unfortunately.

Genesis 3:3 "But of the fruit of the tree which is in the midst of the garden, God hath said, Ye shall not eat of it, neither shall ye touch it, lest ye die."

Very few verses of Scripture have been as discussed as this one, I would venture to guess. "Neither shall ye touch" is one point of discussion. Obviously, in Chapter 2 this part of the command is never given. So, did Adam add to Scripture in telling this to Eve? Unlikely, since adding to the Bible is sin, and that was not the first sin. Did Eve just make that up? No, that would be lying, and lying was not the first sin. Was Eve mistaken? In her perfect state? Highly unlikely in a state of perfection. The most likely explanation is that it was an unrecorded commandment. Just because something is not recorded in Scripture does not mean it did not happen. This is known as the argument from silence. Many things in Scripture occurred but are unmentioned. Noah knew the difference between clean and unclean animals centuries before it was explained in the Law. Sacrifice was known to Cain, Abel, and Noah, but not explained yet in Scripture. This is something to bear in mind as one reads Scripture.

So evidently God told them not to touch the fruit, or they would die. Abstain from all appearance of evil comes to mind. Now other questions arise. Did animals partake of the tree of life? Was it necessary to partake of it in a sinless state, since only by sin comes death? Did the command not to eat of the tree of the knowledge of good and evil extend to animals (likely – As an understanding of headship is seemingly helpful here)?

A few other points to ponder. Did the fruit of the tree grow continually? Or were there seasons at this point for growing? And what happened to this tree? Was it destroyed in the Flood? Or did it die for lack of upkeep after the Fall, when the entrance to it was guarded by the flaming sword? This fruit, in any case, in perfection, must have been quite beautiful.

Another thing to consider, are Eve's words "lest ye die." "Ye" is plural, so the 3 times it is spoken in this verse, is clear that this was a time when God spoke to Adam and Eve both. It could be argued that "lest" is less emphatic than ye shall die. It is a point worth examining.

Another point to ponder is Eve's usage of the words "in the midst of the garden." We have no idea how big the garden was. But we do know it was known to Eve.

Genesis 3:4 "And the serpent said unto the woman, Ye shall not surely die:"

The serpent speaks to Eve in the plural as well, saying "ye shall not surely die." That, along with verse 6, makes it highly likely that Adam was with her. Satan, being a liar from the beginning, is lying to them. He was also a murderer. Think about it. Because of his infernal influence every species of material life has died. Billions upon billions of deaths, trees, flora, fauna, birds, fish, animals, and humans have died because of that lying murderer. John 8:44 says, "Ye are of your father the devil, and the lusts of your father ye will do. He was a murderer from the beginning, and abode not in the truth, because there is no truth in him. When he speaketh a lie, he speaketh of his own: for he is a liar, and the father of it."

The serpent spoke a total of 46 words to Eve. That old serpent, the tempter, satan, lucifer, the accuser of the brethren speaks. He had no weapon but his voice. Eve had all the power at her disposal. But he went for the weakest link to Adam, Eve. Eve listened to a lie, but in consequence the Truth, Jesus would come. She did evil, as did Adam, but Good came. Since God in His foreknowledge knew that Eve would listen, that she and Adam would eat, and sin would come into the world, is that causation? Predestination? No, it is God's foreknowledge. It is God's mercy creating a plan of love and redemption. We are not puppets on a string. The entire purpose of the tree of knowledge of good and evil was for choice and freewill. So, we are not puppets on a string. God wants love from choice, not coercion. Can coercion ever really be love?

Angels fell, one-third of them according to Revelation 12. Why didn't God create a plan of salvation for them? Spirits do not have flesh and blood, so no blood could be shed for them? I really have no idea why God did not create a plan of salvation for fallen angels outside of God's sovereign choice. According to Ephesians 2 we are to be in the ages to come for God to show in us His great mercy.

Notice again the subtilty of the devil. "Surely" is put into the equation. Yet doubt ensues. He could have said ye shall not die, an emphatic statement. But he did not. He said there is a chance you will not die. That leads to a couple of life lessons. First, satan is a liar. Do not listen to him. He can ensnare you. He has been doing this for over 6,000 years. If he could cause one-third of the angels in heaven to fall, he is a master at doubt and deception. And life lesson Number Two is, satan is so evil, he wants every being with cognition to spend eternity in hell with him. He even wanted non-cognitive things such as plants to die. All suffering, death, and pain is directly his fault.

He does not want your good. He wants your eternal torment. He is unadulterated evil. He is the cause there is a hell.

Eve did not seem shocked she was speaking to a serpent. Balaam some 2,500 years later did not seem too startled to be speaking to a donkey, either. Satan did not go after Adam directly here. He seemed to be going for the proverbial weak link. He probably knew the best path to Adam was through Eve.

Just how did satan get into the garden anyway? Was this serpent one of the animals God specially created on day 6, and satan as a spirit possessed it? Or was there a free flow of animals in and out of the garden? Could other animals be possessed by satan at this time as well? Or was this a physical manifestation of the spirit satan? That is why this Commentary is called Discussions in Scripture. Knowledge often comes as we humbly discuss things. In the multitude of counsel, there is wisdom.

Satan's use of the term "ye" may indicate that Adam was within earshot. Satan was speaking to Eve, but Adam could hear as well, possibly. Or satan may have just been speaking to the Woman indicating her oneness with Adam. The same result would be upon both.

Genesis 3:5 "For God doth know that in the day ye eat thereof, then your eyes shall be opened, and ye shall be as gods, knowing good and evil."

Let us unpack this. What "eyes" will be opened? Does this have something to do with the esoteric third eye, which some associate with the pineal gland? Did Adam and Eve have skin over their eyes, and everything was sensory to them before this? Evidently not, as we read further. "Eyes" for a new dimension, in this case sin, as opposed to innocence? Let us examine everything the serpent is offering here.

First, the serpent challenges God's Word. God said in the day you eat thereof you shall surely die. Satan says in the day you eat, your eyes will be opened. This is a direct challenge to God's Word. He is saying God is a liar, not him. Again, what eyes? It seems something beyond the sensory. They were already in the image of God. Except in the realm of sin, they may have already known more than satan, though man was created a little lower than the angels. The only further knowledge they lacked was in the realm of evil. Sin and death. Holiness and innocence should have been their eternal existence. There are some things not worth knowing.

Secondly, satan was offering them that they already had. They were in the image of God. Satan constantly offers us more which really, is far less. We have the greatest life. Life with Jesus is complete. We are complete in Him. Yet satan wants it to be Jesus plus other things. When we get God's water, we will never thirst again. Jesus is the great fulfillment of our lives.

Third, they already knew "good." God is the essence and definition of good. And evil they did not need. But curiosity killed the cat. Pandora, metaphorically, could not keep the box closed. And as an aside, there does seem to be echoes of Genesis in some of the Grecian myths.

Notice the certainty with which the serpent spake. It was definitive. He spake as if he knew for sure. That voice of authority still is used to deceive people today. Discussing things online with people, I have noticed that certain people can write authoritatively, convincingly. And so often, I unfortunately fall prey to it. I get defensive. I think their point is the truth. But when, with God's help, I strip back the voice, it is like the Wizard of Oz. It turns out to be a tremendous bluff, with no or very little truth behind it. Be careful with the voice of authority with no truth behind it.

Satan's accusatory nature is also on full display here against God. You just thought God gave you everything. He is holding back on you, the cad. There is a God conspiracy afoot. God, Who I will not let you consider created this tree, knows you will be enlightened when you partake thereof. Adam and Eve would know evil all too well, but too late. The deceiver would deceive. The snake would lure its prey.

So satan meant to accuse God and confuse Eve. There is only One God. Satan was offering polytheism, a trinity if you will, incorporating Adam and Eve into godhood. It was not to be. All satan's promises have worms.

Genesis 3:6 "And when the woman saw that the tree was good for food, and that it was pleasant to the eyes, and a tree to be desired to make one wise, she took of the fruit thereof, and did eat, and gave also unto her husband with her; and he did eat."

First Eve sees the tree is good for food. Notice she did not just see the fruit was beautiful. She saw that it was good for food. Before we delve into that, I need to post a particular Scripture for further Biblical context.

"For all that is in the world, the lust of the flesh, and the lust of the eyes, and the pride of life, is not of the Father, but is of the world." 1 John 2:16. We see from this New Testament passage that everything in the world's system (that which comes from man), parallels the temptation in the Garden.

Satan ate the fruit. The prohibition was to Adam and Eve. They were in innocence. Satan was in sin. So, this tree was evidently available to him. That seems to be the clear meaning of the first phrase in Genesis 3:6. Notice as well, satan promised to open the woman's eyes. But Eve could already see. And she could already see all that she really needed to see. So, she saw satan eating the fruit, and he must have made it look delicious. And it was, probably. To the palate, anyway. But of course, it would make the stomach bitter. We still do not know what kind of fruit it was. Of course, long tradition says an apple, but that is not certain. But we do know that it was forbidden.

Next, the Woman saw the fruit was pleasant to her eyes. So satan ate it in front of her. She saw it was delicious. She saw it was beautiful as well. Why didn't she run? Where was Adam? Why didn't he stop her? There is a pleasure of sin for a season (Hebrews 11:25).

Wisdom is brought to the fore here. But not God's wisdom. What type of things was satan speaking to her to make her think this was desired to make one wise? Unrecorded in Scripture, there had to be a causative mechanism that Eve saw where she knew it made one wise. Wise in this context means knowledge she did not possess. Forbidden fruit syndrome. She desired it. Wise as serpents as Jesus spoke about. Of her own free will she ate of it. She took of the fruit thereof.

Would this disobedience have been enough to bring sin into the world? What if she would have merely touched it, but not Adam, what then? There are a few paths down that rabbit hole. All of them lead to the fact, that is not what happened. She did touch it, she did eat of it, and she did give to Adam, and he ate of it.

Freewill carried risk. When we raise our children, freewill has risk. But that is the price for free moral agents choosing to love or not. Who wants forced love? Or is that even love at all?

She ate of it. She internalized it. It entered her digestive tract. It became one with her. And the results have been passed down to us. The beautiful perfect DNA had been contaminated.

Now we learn with certainty where Adam has been during this temptation process. With Eve, or as Scripture says, with her. Some make Adam the hero of this story. Many of the Tragedians echo back to this initial cataclysm. The heroic Adam image some portray goes like this. Adam saw his bride sin. He could not stand the thought of losing his bride to death, while he lived in eternal life. So, he died to join her. Since he was in the image of God that is the reaction that God had to us in the Person of Jesus Christ. And if Adam being sinless would have shed his blood instead of dying spiritually with her, he would have redeemed her. There are some holes in this thinking, however.

Adam died with Eve, not for Eve. So, the difference between Adam's death and Jesus' death could not be starker. Adam's act is seen as an act of rebellion. Jesus' death is seen as obedience. Adam's act displeased the Father, Jesus' act satisfied the Father. Adam's act brought sin and death into the world, while Jesus' sacrifice brought life to us. Adam's act was selfish, Jesus' was sacrificial. The two acts of Adam and Jesus are diametrically opposed. The results are polar opposites. As much as I have friends that really buy into the Adam good guy theory, I must stand opposed. Adam opened the door to hell for billions. Not satan, and not even Eve did this. It was Adam that stood guilty of opening the floodtide of evil and hell into this existence for mankind. Adam was not deceived, according to Scripture, but sinned willingly. If Adam wanted to save Eve, why didn't He cry out to God for wisdom on how to do that? No, he was taken in rebellion against God. The same serpent who had deceived one third of the angels worked his deceptive tactics on Adam, and Adam fell for it. And people still do. Most. Almost all. Very few are saved. Satan has so many tactics. We have God. That is enough.

In the most tragic chapter in human history, this is the most devastating passage. In a few short chews of forbidden fruit, mankind devolves. This is the true descent of man.

Let us examine the destructive force of temptation. Having already been weakened by satan's lies and innuendos against God, next Eve "sees." Had she never looked on the fruit before? "Flee fornication" is an admonition of Scripture, as is "flee idolatry." While this was not fornication (but it could possibly be idolatry), Eve should have either fled or taken dominion. But she looked. We also see in this Passage the power of others. She listens to satan. She sees him eat and watches him touch the fruit. So, she does likewise. How often does this power of the other's actions influence us? This fruit looked beautiful. But it was surrounded by orders of magnitude more beauty. Satan's tactic is to get us to focus on the one thing, instead of the many blessings of God. Temporal pleasure and eternal damnation, or the eternal blessings of the Almighty. The choice should be easy. And it was far too easy, in the wrong direction. Unfortunately, that is still so true today. Evil communications still corrupt good manners.

Satan's goal was to get the image of God in hell. He could not defeat God. This was his next best thing. He had deceived 1/3 of the angels. Now he condemned the very innocent, image of God Himself.

The Scripture seems to indicate that Eve took the fruit off the tree, rather than satan handing it to her. The key to this entire episode is that Eve should not have been talking to satan in the first place. There are certain voices we should not interact with. This is one of many lessons God is trying to teach us during this devastating ordeal. She also should not have been near the tree.

Eve touched the fruit. Then she ate of it. She was defiled within and without. This is satan's goal, our total defilement. Satan knows Scripture. Surely, he knew of God's plan for man. Or did he? Was it hidden? Did God only allow angels to see Scripture as it was being written on earth, and not the forever settled copy in heaven? 1 Corinthians 2 says if the princes of this world would have known, they would have never crucified the Lord of glory. Yet an angel in Daniel 10:21 says as it is noted in the Scripture of truth. So, he knew. Regardless, 4 of the saddest words in the Universe are found here, "...and he did eat." 4 syllables, 12 letters, a world destroyed. Satan seeks to defile us inside and out. Jesus cleanses us inside and out.

Genesis 3:7 "And the eyes of them both were opened, and they knew that they were naked; and they sewed fig leaves together, and made themselves aprons."

Their eyes were opened, just as satan had promised. And they knew good and evil, just as satan said. But it was bad, and not good. They didn't become as gods; the image of God became mortal. Satan's promises, then as now, bring the invert of the promise. This one night stand will liberate you, whispers the tempter. This toke will set you free. But it brings enslavement instead.

Much is written on the spiritual implications of nakedness here. I think the plain teaching of physical nakedness and the beginnings of modesty are many times overlooked. I think this is one of the greatest mistakes in Biblical interpretation, missing the plain meaning looking for a deeper meaning. I have friends who cannot read Revelation Chapters 2 and 3 without seeing Church ages. In my understanding, they are missing amazing, valuable, God-given lessons of seven angels and churches that God is giving there. And if we are the continuation of the apostolic church, these lessons are for us as well. They are seven other short epistles to go with the other 21 in the New Testament and have ministry toward us as the other Epistles do. So, we can miss the obvious for the esoteric.

And this is obvious. One of the immediate effects of eating the forbidden fruit was a realization of nakedness. Physical nakedness. Physical nakedness now brings shame. Before this they were naked and not ashamed. There is a natural desire for covering in mankind. Modesty and covering are a Biblical issue. And a spiritual issue. This was the first, immediate result of the Fall of mankind. Their eyes were opened, and they knew they were naked. This tree of knowledge let them know they were naked. Skin is an attractant. Mankind's fallen nature will lust after skin. David lusted after naked skin. Jesus said if you look upon a woman to lust after her, you have committed adultery in your heart already. Biblical cultures, like Israel and the West of yesteryear, covered themselves due to this Biblical principle. And it is not just a Biblical principle, there is something inherent in man that lets us know this. Clothing is not evolutionary. It is not predicated on convenience. It is Biblical. Modesty is not some backburner doctrine. It is front and center. It is internal in humans. Of course, the New Birth is preeminent. But modesty is part of holiness. The demoniac was naked. When he was delivered, he was clothed and in his right mind.

Adam and the woman here sew fig leaves together. They realize they are naked. When immodestly dressed people are in the presence of Spirit-filled people, many times they begin to unconsciously cover themselves or get uncomfortable. This is not judgmentalness, it is conviction. Needle and thread? Evidently. And that would indicate that their culture did not just occur that day. This was evidently not a continuation of Day Six, as much of Chapter 2 was. But they must have been in there long enough to have needle and thread unless they invented it just for this. But it is much more plausible that they invented it in their excelled state before the Fall. Or God had given it to them at some unmentioned time. And since their first sin was not disobeying the command to be fruitful and multiply, they probably had children in the interregnum. Randomly, I wonder again if Adam and Eve could travel outside of the garden. I would say yes if their dominion extended over all the earth. Since the moon is the earth's gravitational sphere, could they go there as well? I have no idea.

"Aprons" indicate partial and not full covering. God would make them better clothes later. Man's fallen fashion is still not sufficient. We should seek God for our clothing choices.

Spiritual eyes were opened. Eve had been tempted through physical eyes. The beauty of the physical world had been darkened. The contagion of death loosed. Entropy, the Second Law of Thermodynamics, enters the once perfect earth. Innocence had been violated. Their attempt at omniscience had failed. They learned new things, but only tragic new things. Such as what death was, destruction, failure, depression, and the like. Yes, they saw things they wished they had not.

Temptation in man still hearkens back to this event. Man, at that time begins evolving downward, not upward. Ancient technologies, architecture, astronomy, mathematics, the pyramids, and such like show us man was not originally troglodytes. The pyramids remain. Will any of our structures remain 3-4,000 years from now? Temptation brought sin. Sin brought death and degradation, a general despondency in the human species. So-called missing links are non-existent. Sin caused mankind to go downward, not upward. But even in the midst of the ultimate tragedy, God offers hope.

Genesis 3:8 "And they heard the voice of the LORD God walking in the garden in the cool of the day: and Adam and his wife hid themselves from the presence of the LORD God amongst the trees of the garden."

The voice of the LORD God was walking. Now this could mean that Adam and Eve were walking, and they heard the voice of God. But it could also mean that the voice (The Word) of God, the visible form of God Himself, was walking in the Garden. This certainly seems to be how the Text reads. And this comports with John 1:1-14, along with several other portions of Scripture.

Another fascinating aspect is found here. There was a cool of the day. We do not know if this was caused supernaturally for Adam and Eve's pleasure, or is this just meaning a particular time of day? I have heard various interpretations.

The voice of the LORD God is here identified as the presence of the LORD God. Notice it is not a separate person from God. Your word is you, not a separate person. And you are in the image of God. This certainly fits with the monotheism of Scripture, that God is an absolute One, not a composite One. God is a Spirit, John 4:24. And the Presence of God caused Adam and the woman to hide themselves among the trees. The trees were for food. Sin makes them for hiding. A tree will one day be used as a tool to bring redemption. Leaves from a tree do a poor job of hiding nakedness. The fruit on Calvary's tree brings an end to sin and shame. Cursed is everyone who hangs on a tree. Jesus became sin, so we could be sinless. He set us free. But this process of conviction continues to this day. When we are in the presence of God, and we are in sin, we are convicted. We try to hide from the presence of the LORD. God is holy. Sometimes when we do not want to go to Church, it is not the Church's fault, we just do not want to be in the Presence of a Holy God. God's Presence, His Holiness, brings conviction.

We should run to God when we sin. Instead, like the first couple, we often hide. God is our Savior. He is the only source of forgiveness. He is our only hope. Yet still like Adam and Eve we hide, rather than run to Him. We are ashamed.

Many have postulated that this was a regular meeting place with God, in the cool of the day. Some may even posit that the cool of the day was 9 a.m., when the Spirit fell on Pentecost. All of this is speculation. It may be true, but I see no way of proving it is or it is not. It certainly should not be preached as doctrine unless there is further evidence.

Genesis 3:9 "And the LORD God called unto Adam, and said unto him, Where art thou?"

Satan has been speaking, now God speaks. Holy Adam could get close to the serpent, but he hides from God. How often do we talk with the devil instead of God? How many times are we worldly, listening to the devil's temptation, when we should be with God?

Jehovah Elohim calls to Adam. Jesus said if He be lifted up, He would draw all men unto Himself. He is the True Light that lighteth every man that comes into the world. What an act of mercy. Man, in his rebellion and sin is called by Almighty God. Jesus, God in Flesh, came to seek and to save that which was lost. His Spirit is still calling to lost humanity.

God begins to ask questions. Being omniscient, knowing everything, He already knew the answer to the questions. His purpose seems to be to make them, and us, confront uncomfortable truths. He is guiding us to expose ourselves, and then to confess and repent. Godly sorrow leads to repentance not to be repented of. God here calls unto Adam. Now this could either be that Adam and the woman at this point had 1 name, Adam, because they were one flesh (5:2). Or it could be God was making headship answer first. The use of "thou" indicates it is the latter.

"Called" is a theological concept. We see in 2:19 that Adam called the animals by name. Here God calls Adam by name. In the New Testament, we call on God's name for salvation, and we have His Name called over us in baptism.

Adam knew where he was at physically. But did he have any idea of his spiritual state? What must the feeling have felt like when he first lost immortality as the fruit slid down his throat? Adam was lost. Not physically, though he was trying to hide from God, but spiritually. From the exquisite penultimate joy of perfection and fellowship with God, to the lowly, sinful state of sin. The descent of man indeed.

Genesis 3:10 "And he said, I heard thy voice in the garden, and I was afraid, because I was naked; and I hid myself."

We hear Adam speaking for the first time as an unsaved man. Naked and ashamed. God, who should bring joy, now brings fear. Perfect love casteth out fear. So now perfect love between 2 perfect beings has been sundered. Adam speaks 19 words here. He gives the reason for his fear as his nakedness. We see how modesty is supposed to work. When a society is full of God, it dresses holy. When it degenerates, and there is no fear of God before its eyes, nakedness creeps back in. But it is not the innocent nakedness as in the beginning. It is a nakedness tainted by sin that leads to horrible things due to the sinful nature of mankind.

Adam could still hear God's voice. This is a theme of Scripture. Hearing God's voice does not necessarily mean we are right with God. When God began to speak with Cain, Adam's son, in the next chapter, it was immediately after he had failed and sinned. There have been times of failure and sin in my life. And so often it is then I hear the voice of God the loudest. Not in approval, but in chastisement and direction for mercy.

Leaves could not hide Adam's nakedness. The trees of the garden could not. Only God could. And I wonder if there was a significance of the leaves being figs? When Jesus wanted figs on a tree during his Passion Week and they were lacking, He cursed the fig tree. Many think that the fig tree was a type of Israel or the Law. Maybe a typology that our attempts at righteousness are not accepted? Since there is nothing accidental or incidental in Scripture, and the Scripture names the tree, I am sure there is a significance. I have never studied the significance, however to any great degree. Also, some have said the fruit of the tree of knowledge was fig, since Adam sewed fig leaves together. Maybe, but I am certainly not sure of that. Jewish theology thinks it was a loaf of bread.

Fruit and leaves are an extension of the wood in a tree. That would be a fascinating typology to examine at some point. Jesus hung on a tree (cross). Leaves could not cover properly. Fruit brought both life and death depending on the tree it came from. So much there.

Adam's response in this verse is lamentable. From dominion to hiding. From fellowship with the Creator to fear. From naked and not ashamed to clothed insufficiently and afraid.

Genesis 3:11 "And he said, Who told thee that thou wast naked? Hast thou eaten of the tree, whereof I commanded thee that thou shouldest not eat?"

God follows up a question, with two more questions. He who rests needing not rest, also asks questions already knowing the answer. In God's dealings with Adam, I am reminded of David, a man after God's own heart, crying out about his son, "Absalom, Absalom, O my son Absalom." God still comes to seek and to save that which was lost. And He is here asking Adam questions, not to get Adam to be even more ashamed so much, but to acknowledge his own guilt so he can be saved.

God here speaks 22 words. He asked two questions. So many of us had parents that would do the same thing. We would be caught doing something we were not supposed to do. Yet our parents would ask, did you do that? Confession is good for the soul.

Notice God commanded. God's commandments are not prohibitory to punish us, but rather safety to bless us. Sin kills, holiness gives life. Have you noticed how satan has tried to make holiness a bad word? God is holy, so if you do not like holiness, you can't love God. End of story. Full stop.

In examining God's first question, did anyone have to tell Adam he was naked? Or did he just figure it out? Did satan mock him and tell him? Verse seven shows it was their realization of nakedness. Another observation in this verse is the singular thee and thou in reference to Adam. It sure seems as if God is dealing directly with Adam as a matter of headship. To whom much is given, much is required.

There were so many pleasures and possibilities in Eden. But the "thou shouldest not" caught Adam and catches us. If we could just constantly behold the love, mercy, grace, and power of God, we would be ok. But we constantly want to see what we can get away with, and still be right with God. We truly are adulterers and adulteresses in that sense. David got it right when he said, "Now therefore in the sight of all Israel the congregation of the LORD, and in the audience of our God, keep and seek for all the commandments of the LORD your God: that ye may possess this good land, and leave it for an inheritance for your children after you for ever." In 1 Chronicles 28:8.

We should be trying to see what pleases God that we do not already know about, instead of trying to get away with the grey areas. David also said, "Thou wilt shew me the path of life: in thy presence is fulness of joy; at thy right hand there are pleasures for evermore." in Psalm 16:11. Adam left God's presence of fullness of joy to be slain with the wiles of satan. O Adam!

What horrors were unleashed. Sin always takes us farther than we wanted to go, keeps us longer than we wanted to stay, and makes us pay more than we wanted to pay. Sin affects the world for destruction. Righteousness affects it for salvation and beauty. Holiness has a salt and light effect on the world. We shine as lights in the midst of a crooked and perverse nation.

Genesis 3:12 "And the man said, The woman whom thou gavest to be with me, she gave me of the tree, and I did eat."

Human nature has not changed since Adam's time. When in doubt, blame someone else. Notice the nefarious inference in this blame. It was not just the woman's fault. It was the woman You gave to be with me, she is to blame. Notice not just the woman You gave. But You gave her to be with me. She caused me to do this because I was with her. If only I could have been somewhere else, Adam seems to imply. We see here the use of the word "gave" and "gavest." You gave me the woman. A gift, but now look what she has done. She gave me of the tree, and I did eat. We are reminded of Aaron some 2,500 years or so later, as he stammered to Moses, "And I said unto them, Whosoever hath any gold, let them break it off. So they gave it me: then I cast it into the fire, and there came out this calf." Exodus 32:24. The idea of blame is endemic to mankind. I have known a few correction officers over the years. The testimony of them all is they have almost never met an inmate who said they were guilty. I have pressed them on this issue. They said they ask, and almost all of them, without fail, from the model inmate to all others say they are innocent. Now I am sure there are inmates that acknowledge their guilt. And I am sure there are innocent inmates. But it seems overwhelmingly most do not acknowledge their guilt. Personal responsibility is a wonderful trait, and it is rare.

It is fascinating what God chose to share about Adam. Adam spoke in Chapter 2 and also here. But God chose to leave us in the dark (for now) on what Adam thought about the Cain and Abel scenario in the next chapter. Or his opinion about Cain's descendants. Or Enoch. Or what he thought about sin and death. Self-reflection on how he could have handled things in the Garden differently. His thoughts on life in perfection before the Fall. His last words and thoughts. God must have thought those things unimportant to us for now. And I am fine with that. We have enough to know what God wants for us now. Whatever God chose to share in His Word is sufficient. It is perfect for us.

In Ephesians 5:23 there is an interesting factoid to consider about

Adam. It reads, "For the husband is the head of the wife, even as Christ is the head of the church: and he is the saviour of the body." This indicates that the husband is the savior of the body. It is his responsibility to ensure the spiritual well-being of his family. Could this entire episode really be Adam abdicating his responsibility toward his wife, and failing to exercise his authority over the devil? Another area to consider, is it possible that satan had tried to tempt them before and was rebuffed? And as an aside, did they know he was more subtil than all the beasts of the field?

Job interestingly enough has some fascinating insight about this time period. In Job 31:33 we read, "If I covered my transgressions as Adam, by hiding mine iniquity in my bosom:" Does this indicate Adam hid the uneaten part of the fruit under his clothes? Job 15:7 says rhetorically, again possibly in reference to Adam, "Art thou the first man that was born? or wast thou made before the hills?" Zophar knew man was placed upon earth, when he said, "Knowest thou not this of old, since man was placed upon earth," Job 20:4. Job 10:11 gives fascinating insight about man, "Thou hast clothed me with skin and flesh, and hast fenced me with bones and sinews."

I notice too that Adam avoided mentioning the fruit. He also obeyed the voice of his wife rather than the voice of God. This is a Biblical theme which continues throughout Scripture. The Adam's apple is so named because supposedly that is where the fruit was when God confronted Adam. And women have a monthly cycle since she ate first, and the fruit had entered her belly. These are ancient traditions which may have some validity.

Genesis 3:13 "And the LORD God said unto the woman, 'What is this that thou hast done? And the woman said, The serpent beguiled me, and I did eat.'"

Jehovah Elohim concludes speaking with the man for now and begins to speak with the woman. Notice God began by speaking to Adam. Satan began by speaking to Eve. The woman here speaks 8 words. And she appears to be speaking truth. In 1 Timothy 2:14 we see that. "And Adam was not deceived, but the woman being deceived was in the transgression." So, Eve was deceived. And she was in transgression. Transgression is "parabasis" in Greek, and it is a breaking or breach of well-defined law. So, Eve was deceived, or "beguiled" as it is here in Genesis. But Adam was not. He ate of his own volition. Maybe he did not want to be unequally yoked with an unbeliever. Possibly he wanted to maintain with his own kind. Whatever the case was, he was in rebellion. But Eve was a transgressor as well.

Eve spoke in the immediate. Maybe I should say the woman that will soon be called Eve. What had she done? Destroyed the world. Job 25:5 says, "Behold even to the moon, and it shineth not; yea, the stars are not pure in his sight." Job 15:15 says, "Behold, he putteth no trust in his saints; yea, the heavens are not clean in his sight." It is almost as if this defilement extended into the heavens. If the heavens were created predicated upon the earth, this could very well be so. And if hell is in the center of the earth, Job 28:5 may indicate as such, when it says, "As for the earth, out of it cometh bread: and under it is turned up as it were fire."

You will notice there is a great affinity between Genesis, especially from the Flood and before, and Job. These events must have been emblazoned upon the minds of the righteous ancients. Job is a book written not too long after the Flood of Noah. Mythologies arose among the pagans as they looked back at these events and they were corrupted in their thinking.

The Voice of the LORD walking in the garden has spoken. And He asks questions. And He is speaking to us. He is trying to get us to avoid our appointed date with an eternal hell. Eve must have been feeling emotions she had never felt before. Fear, shame, conviction, and the like. Her eyes had been opened, and it was unpleasant. And as we shall see in the next verse, it appears the serpent was still near her, even after she and Adam had hidden themselves.

Genesis 3:14 "And the LORD God said unto the serpent, 'Because thou hast done this, thou art cursed above all cattle, and above every beast of the field; upon thy belly shalt thou go, and dust shalt thou eat all the days of thy life:'"

As mentioned previously, it appears that the serpent was close by. This is not definite, however. But possibly this unholy triumvirate were now together. Adam and Eve were convicted, ashamed. The serpent however, full of pride, seems to have been able to come directly into the presence of God with no shame, just as in Job 1 and 2. Being shameless in a sense, is not good. But of course, he fears. James 2:19 records, "Thou believest that there is one God; thou doest well: the devils also believe, and tremble. "So, when that lying spirit came before the Throne to deceive Ahab, he was trembling. When satan came together with the sons of God in Job 1 and 2, he was trembling. And he was probably trembling here as well. Could he have been filled with a sense of glee also? The devils that Jesus confronted would run toward him, but they certainly did not want to get tormented before their time.

We also see that God did not bother asking the serpent any questions. Notice God had spent Chapters 1 and 2 in blessing. Now he curses. As far as not having a dialogue with satan, maybe this is instructive. Jesus did ask Legions' name. But possibly we should follow this example and highly limit conversations with the serpent. Just speak to him in the Name of Jesus, and let God do the rest. We see that the curse would extend to all cattle and the beast of the field, but the serpent's curse would be worse than theirs. Going on his belly, rather than upright one would assume, would be the ultimate in humbling this creature of pride. And eating dust would seem to be humbling as well. Adam was created from dust. Possibly this was to be a reminder of what satan had done to the dust of God. It also seems that this curse would be in perpetuity, extending to offspring, just as the curse on man and other animals would be.

The relationship between satan and the serpent is interesting. Again, just as devils inhabited hogs in the NT, it seems that satan possessed this serpent. Maybe serpents and all animals had far more intelligence then than now. So maybe the serpent knew better than to have satan possess him but allowed it anyway. We do know that satan is referred to as that old serpent in Revelation 12:9, and Revelation 20:2. That has a direct correlation to this narrative. Just as we have Theophany's, maybe this was a "satanophany," so to speak.

The reason the other animals were cursed in their innocence is 2-fold, seemingly. The first is their head, Adam, had sinned. And this shows us the enormous responsibilities of leadership. Seventy thousand Israelites lost their lives because King David numbered the people in sin. Revelation 2 and 3 show the angels' influence over each of the seven churches of Asia, and the angel seems to be a euphemism for some type of ministerial leadership. What responsibilities leaders have! There may be more to the anointing flowing downward as in Psalm 133 than some realize.

There was a moment in time when Adam and Eve were fallen, and the curse had not yet been pronounced, and the serpent still stood. But judgment came. In our lives we may sin, and just because the judgment does not come like Ananias and Sapphira, it does not mean that judgement is not coming. It is. Unless we confess and forsake our sins (Proverbs 28:13).

The beautiful fruit was poison, and the serpent was to eat of the cursed earth along with his progeny. A change in DNA had taken place throughout the entire earth. The suns UV rays would begin the process of death instead of only life.

This brings us to a theology of angels and demons. I believe all devils are fallen angels, who fell sometime in eternity past. Other points of view would say, yes this is correct for some, but some humans who die also come back as devils. Others say that may or may not be true, but there are at least one more class of devils. And these would be the sons of God found in Genesis 6. We will discuss that more, LORD willing, later.

Genesis 3:15 "And I will put enmity between thee and the woman, and between thy seed and her seed; it shall bruise thy head, and thou shalt bruise his heel."

God continues to speak to lucifer here. God spoke a total of 63 words to him. I am here assuming that lucifer and satan are the same being. Some do not feel this is the case. My reasons for thinking that are too long for the current treatise. So, God here says that enmity will be between the serpent and the woman. They will no longer be together but separated. And this is true. Many women have an aversion to snakes, more so than men. But it does not stop there. The serpent is going to have a seed. This does not refer to satan as a spirit making love to women and having offspring. This refers to people who follow the serpent's ways and not God's. And the woman is going to have a seed. Normally the man has a seed. But this seems to be a direct prophecy of the virgin birth, when a woman compasses a man (Jeremiah 31:22). And this seed of the woman, the Messiah, Jesus, was going to be at war with the seed of satan. Now some say that just as Jesus as the seed is singular, so the serpent's seed would be singular as well. So, this would be referring to the antichrist, the beast of revelation. John 8:44 would be instructive to look at here, as it says "Ye are of your father the devil, and the lusts of your father ye will do. He was a murderer from the beginning, and abode not in the truth, because there is no truth in him. When he speaketh a lie, he speaketh of his own: for he is a liar, and the father of it." This is speaking of the Pharisees. Again, they are not the offspring of satan. They just followed him. God so loved the world. Jesus died for their sins. Paul, a Pharisee, became a great Apostle. But God is also at war with them in their rejection of Him. It is possible to be at war with an enemy and ask him to surrender at the same time.

This seed of the woman, the Messiah, would bruise satan's head. But the belly dwelling dust eater would bruise Jesus' heel. This seems a clear reference to the nail through the heel at the Crucifixion of Christ. Also, this enmity between the woman and the serpent. I wonder if this is where praying women come in? And does hair, and "because of the angels" fit in here somewhere?

Eve would have presumably had some type of fellowship with serpents in the Garden. Was this serpent different? We must ask, was this serpent satan in physical form, or a serpent possessed by satan? That is a fascinating question.

Romans 16:20 does fit this verse as well. It reads, "And the God of peace shall bruise Satan under your feet shortly. The grace of our Lord Jesus Christ be with you. Amen." The context of this verse is verse 19, and it does bear some resemblance of the events happening in Genesis Two and Three. It reads thusly, "For your obedience is come abroad unto all men. I am glad therefore on your behalf: but yet I would have you wise unto that which is good, and simple concerning evil." Notice the prerequisite for the Church at Rome bruising satan under their feet. Obedience is first. Then wise unto that which is good, and simple concerning evil. The tree in the garden was of the knowledge of good and evil. God here tells us for victory we need knowledge (wisdom) of the good, but simplicity of the evil. So, God did not want us to have the knowledge of good and evil, only the good. He does say be wise as serpents as well, however. Now mankind not only has conscience, knowledge of the good (but also of wrong) according to Romans, but a sinful nature and a wicked heart, or knowledge of evil as well. A sinful nature has been saddled upon mankind. When saved, we are part of the Body of Christ. So, we participate in Christ's victory.

Genesis 3:16 "Unto the woman he said, I will greatly multiply thy sorrow and thy conception; in sorrow thou shalt bring forth children; and thy desire shall be to thy husband, and he shall rule over thee."

God now speaks to the woman. He says He will multiply, but not in the blessing sense of Chapter 1. Rather, He would multiply the woman's sorrow. Interestingly, Jesus would be known as a man of sorrows. God would also multiply her conception. This seems to be a reference to extending the gestation period. Before the Fall, childbirth seems to have been much quicker. One would assume with unfallen reproductive systems; every act of sexual intimacy would result in childbirth. And the indication is that the woman had already experienced that. Maybe daily, we just do not know. So, Adam and Eve had obeyed God and were fruitful and multiplying before this tragic event happened. How many children they had, or how quick the gestation period was pre-Fall, we just do not know. But these children would be great candidates for the sons of God in Genesis 6. See Luke 3:38 and Genesis 5:3 for further elucidation on this matter. Another Scripture in Romans may be instructive here as well, but not necessarily. Romans 5:14 "Nevertheless death reigned from Adam to

Moses, even over them that had not sinned after the similitude of Adam's transgression, who is the figure of him that was to come."

Nine months, and then a near death experience or worse is part of the curse for women, in bearing children. But it does not stop there. The woman's desire will be to her husband. Was it not before? Evidently not in this way. Women would want a man's attention, and would want to please her husband, evidently in a distorted way. Instead of being a help, more of a submissive. My language fails me in trying to adequately communicate this. See Ephesians 5, 1 Corinthians 11, and 1 Peter 3 for more discussion points. The initial relationship of Adam and the woman seems to have been more of a partnership. But now the man will rule over the woman. Not a help meet for him, but more of a hierarchy of order. Something not originally intended by God, at least in a sense. Of course, headship was Adam's original design, so again, preciseness of language fails me.

Genesis 3:17 "And unto Adam he said, Because thou hast hearkened unto the voice of thy wife, and hast eaten of the tree, of which I commanded thee, saying, Thou shalt not eat of it: cursed is the ground for thy sake; in sorrow shalt thou eat of it all the days of thy life;"

After speaking to man, woman, then the serpent, God then goes to woman, then the man in His pronouncement of judgment. Notice this judgment was not just on the man and woman, but on all their offspring, and the entire created order as well. And God has a direct confrontation with Adam on the nature of his sin. He says Adam hearkened unto the voice of his wife. This is not recorded in the Scriptural narrative, per se. It does not say Eve spoke with Adam, just that she gave to him. But here we find that she spoke with him. God had spoken to Adam in Genesis 2. That Voice, which was God, walked in the garden after the Fall. Jesus has a Name written on His vesture in Revelation 19, the Word of God. He is the Word, John 1 and 1 John 1. That was the pre-incarnate Jesus in the Garden, the Father of Glory. So, God's first observation is that Adam hearkened to Eve's voice over His. How many voices do we hearken to besides God's? This is still man's basic problem. We listen to ourselves, our traditions, our culture, our society, others, sin, demons, and temptation, more than we listen to God's Word.

So, he ate of the tree, which God had commanded him not to. God still commands us about things today. It is not legalism or fleshly law. It is His way and His prerogative. Will you humble yourself to obey God's Voice? This is the essence of holiness.

The serpent is to eat of the cursed ground, the dust. Now the ground from which Adam was taken is cursed. So, the serpent is to partake of cursed ground as he slithers on his belly. And sorrow is not just the purview of the woman. Adam is to partake of that as well. For Adam to eat, instead of the plenteousness of the Garden, he would have to work through a cursed ground, with weeds, thorns, and brambles. He would sweat and bleed, just as the last Adam would do 4,000 years or so later, for our redemption. There would be no retirement. If Adam were to eat, he was to work. The contrast with the grace of God in the Garden could not be clearer. Work went from purpose and pleasure to life gnawing necessity. Every incredible food had been given to Adam by God's grace. Now Adam would be working in the field to feed his family, as Eve would be busy and sorrowing in pregnancy and child rearing. The way of transgressor's is certainly hard (Proverbs 13:15).

Adam, as is clear from the New Testament, is at the core of the great Fall. We sometimes call it the Fall of man. But the domino effect destroyed so much more, and increased hell in the process. In the Law we read that a man could invalidate the vow of his wife. I am not sure if that would have applied in Adam's situation at the tree of knowledge. What I am sure of is that Adam did not disannul Eve's disobedient deception, but rather ratified it. So, in Genesis 3:17 we have God going back over Adam's sin. Like a Judge reading the sentence. Accusation and guilt come first, then the punishment. Reproof then correction. It is striking that Adam literally left his Father and his mother (New Jerusalem, or Jerusalem that is above), and clave to his wife, just as he prophesied in Chapter 2.

The ground was no longer blessed but cursed. Adam came from the ground. The tree of life, and the tree of knowledge, grew in the ground. The serpent was to slither on the ground. And Adam was to till the ground. A fascinating fact is that the ground is no longer cursed. The Flood, which is a type of water baptism, symbolically cleansed it. In Genesis 8:21 it says, "And the LORD smelled a sweet savour; and the LORD said in his heart, I will not again curse the ground any more for man's sake; for the imagination of man's heart is evil from his youth; neither will I again smite any more every thing living, as I have done." So, after the Flood, tillage was easier. Possibly the silt nourished the Earth. Cain must have been a hardworking man to till the cursed ground. Maybe he was jealous of Abel due to Abel's perceived less strenuous work of Shepherding. Possibly that contributed to why he was so upset that his offering was not respected by God. Maybe the reason he did not want to give the first and best to God is because the cursed ground caused him to work so hard. He was Adam's firstborn after the Fall and would follow in dad's footsteps as a farmer. But maybe it was not a factor at all.

Four thousand years later a tree would grow, that would be fashioned into a cross. On that cross sinless God and Man would hang for Adam's sin. He would die, be planted, and rise again (1 Corinthians 15 on the newness of the resurrected body of which farming is a type) and all who would eat of Him would have eternal life, not death. The seed would reproduce after His kind. New Creatures, sons, and daughters of Almighty God. A different kind from the fallen world.

Verse 18 "Thorns also and thistles shall it bring forth to thee; and thou shalt eat the herb of the field;"

The pronouncement of the curse continues. God spoke 101 words here in pronouncement of judgement. Thorns could make Adam bleed. Thorns would be on the precious Head of the second Adam. God so made it that with the rose comes thorns. Red beauty surrounded by hurt and pain. The Online Merriam Webster defines thistle thusly: "any of various prickly composite plants (especially genera Carduus, Cirsium, and Onopordum) with often showy heads of mostly tubular flowers. also: any of various other prickly plants." So, the overall throughst of the first part of this verse is pain and sorrow. Adam's farming sorrow and Eve's pregnancy sorrow would produce the man of sorrows, Jesus, who would also be acquainted with grief. Notice God's usage of the singular word "thee." Though the ground was cursed through the period of the Flood to everyone, it began with Adam. These thorns and thistles seem to have been foreign to creation at this time, just based on the sentence structure. "Shall it bring forth to thee" indicates it had not as of yet. Or if they had been, they would have been for beauty and not curse. They would have been only decorative in nature. Did thorns grow after the Fall or before? The wasp's stinger, the spiders bite, the scorpions tail? The claw of the predator, the tooth of the beast? Interesting questions indeed.

Man's diet in these first few days of the Creation epic is an interesting study. In Genesis 1:29 God tells man he can eat of the herb of the ground. Was it of necessity or pleasure or both? In 2:16, God tells man he can also eat of the trees. Now we are back to herbs in this verse. Is it herbs exclusively, or were trees allowed to be eaten (and their fruit)? Or were they off limits because man had sinned by eating from a tree, so now he would have to farm, plow, plant, harvest, process, etc.? I am assuming this is the beginning of crops and agriculture in active cultivation, in a sense. But the overall premise is clear. Man had sinned. And as punishment the food was no longer provided. And it was no longer perfect. Man would have to work for it. But God's creative process and mercy still played a part in the provision. Without His creation and mercy, Adam would die. It would just be more difficult to eat now.

Genesis 3:19 "In the sweat of thy face shalt thou eat bread, till thou return unto the ground; for out of it wast thou taken: for dust thou art, and unto dust shalt thou return."

Had Adam ever sweat before? Or was this something activated after the Fall? A dormant organ awaiting to be awakened at the time of sin, perhaps? God did speak to Adam like Adam was aware of what sweat was. Even in sweat, we see God's mercy. Sweat cools us. Sweat removes impurities from us. The salt in the sweat may remind us of the Fall, but the other attributes remind us of God's love. And Adam would not eat unless he sweat. What type of weather was after the Fall? Possibly it never rained until the Flood. Was it cold? The Bible says in Genesis 1:14 that lights in the firmament were for seasons. We also know that the ice caps were not always covered in ice. The existence of fauna and flora found at the poles buried under the ice shows us that. Other climatic anomalies occur around the world from ancient times.

Death. What a terrible word, awesome in its immensity. Every material living thing dies. Hebrews 2:15 indicates that there is a universal dread in mankind concerning death. It reads, "And deliver them who through fear of death were all their lifetime subject to bondage." Romans says the creation was not subject to death willingly. It groans in pain. God here informs Adam he would return to the ground. Since man is in the image of God, maybe this is hinting at the origin of the practice of burial. Adam, you go back to where you began. Satan promised you that you would be like gods. But you are dust. For dust thou art. Notice God did not say, dust you were, but I made you something different. No, God uses the present tense here. Dust you currently are. And you will return to dust. That is the fate of physical mankind, until the resurrection. All will be resurrected from the dust, both good and evil, saved, and unsaved. Some to everlasting life, others to everlasting torment and death.

Scientists tell us we breathe with every inhale some of the molecules that Jesus breathed. That George Washington breathed, that Caesar breathed, Napoleon and others. There is seemingly an interconnectedness to mankind. I am not sure how much the atmosphere changed after the Fall of man, but I wonder if we breathe the same air that Adam breathed, that Eve breathed. That the serpent breathed.

This is a horrific homage to the curse, from paradise to paradise lost. From life and pleasure to sweat and death. Truly God's justice comes to us all. We must plead for mercy.

Notice this as far as Divine Creation is concerned. Products like wheat must be grown together. They pollinate themselves. They are not isolated. How could multiples of the same plant have evolved at once, at the same location? They could not have, and of course that is just one more of the reasons the theory of evolution is just not true. Even our teeth are an all or nothing proposition. Partial teeth would not suffice to break down food for proper swallowing and digestion. Acids and saliva in proper proportions. There are many such functions in life that show us the impossibility of evolution. Adaptation, yes. But not evolution.

So, to conclude this verse, God was communicating to Adam that it was God and His love, mercy and grace that made Adam anything. Forget that, and it is back to dust for you, an object even smaller than dirt.

Genesis 3:20 "And Adam called his wife's name Eve; because she was the mother of all living."

Adam still had dominion. Adam is still naming, as in Chapter 2. So here he called his wife's name Eve. Notice there was only one wife for Adam. Polygamy was not the original intent. And Adam could name since he was in the image of God. This has great importance in Jesus' Name baptism today. We have the God-given authority to name the name of Jesus over a person. And God gives them His name.

Eve means "life" or "living." If she had indeed had offspring before this time, that is the natural meaning. If not, maybe Eve had a mothering instinct for the animal kingdom. But I think it means the former. But I am still studying that proposition.

It is fascinating that it appears that the oneness between Adam and the woman had disappeared in a sense. In Genesis 5:2 we find they had 1 name, Adam. Now, she has a separate name, Eve. Eve was in Adam. The act of marriage is symbolic of that union of oneness. Women still traditionally take the man's name, though at times, like that in the case of Barzilai's daughters Biblically, the man took the woman's name (Ezra 2:61).

So, Adam was to live 930 years. I assume that all these events took place in year 1 of his life. Some make a point that if God created Adam with the appearance of age, and not just appearance but actually a grown man, then God could have done the same with inorganic matter also. He definitely did with living things, fully formed and fully filled. I still think the entire ancient dating of things is suspect. All the 21 or so types of ancient dating I've seen have variables that are unknowable, and hence could very well be corrupted. There are certain assumptions of the gases and elements, and their previous quantities in rocks, the atmosphere and such like, that are just that, assumptions. There is no evidence of their previous amounts, per se. And the corruption of the Flood, UV rays, differences in the atmosphere etc., and I look at the entire process as quite unreliable. And I am not alone in my assessments.

Adam was to die in the day he ate the fruit. He did not drop dead like Ananias and Sapphira. Death quite possibly has dimensions or stages to it. Death certainly entered his body immediately. His innocence died. His immortality died. And since God is holy, sin separated Adam from God, so as it has been said, Adam died in a sense, spiritually. Paul said this, "And you hath he quickened, who were dead in trespasses and sins;" (Eph. 2:1). So definitely in that sense, Adam died. Some try to say a day is 1,000 years, and he did not live to a 1,000 so that counts as the day. Possibly.

Did animals become carnivorous or omnivorous after the Fall? Certainly, after the Flood. We will see as we continue our journey if Scripture gives the answer to this question.

Genesis 3:21 "Unto Adam also and to his wife did the LORD God make coats of skins, and clothed them."

Some find this one of the most significant verses in Holy Writ. Jehovah Elohim makes Adam and the newly named Eve coats of skins. Blood sacrifice. Animals had to be slain for the animal skins. A few things are in play here. First, it never says animal skins. Gene Edwards in his book the Divine Romance thinks that Adam and Eve, being in the image of God, had no skin before this. God is light and a Spirit. So, they were light, and the Fall brought that death coat of blood and flesh on them, skin. And this would also prefigure Jesus Christ, the Messiah, God in flesh. God would come in flesh to die for us. I personally do not think this is true, but it is fascinating reasoning nonetheless, and at least worthy of consideration.

Next is a modesty consideration. Adam and Eve had fashioned themselves aprons, or as the Geneva Bible so famously puts it, breeches. But fig leaves, being sheer, and from the cursed earth, were not sufficient for covering, only a skin would do. And if it was a sheep, I wonder if that is why we still wear wool today? The shame of nakedness is here at the beginning. Clothing is a public essential, not an option.

But the shedding of blood teaching is still the most significant. God is holy. With sin comes death. So, a substitution was made. A sinless animal shed its blood, as God poured out His wrath upon it instead of the perpetrators. And these are ancient things as Scripture says, and C.S. Lewis agrees to.

Both Adam and Eve needed the blood. In Christ Jesus there is neither male nor female. The same plan of salvation is for both. We stand as individuals before God, not as collective in this sense.

I would be interested in this process. Did God slay the animals in front of Adam and Eve to make them see the heinous nature of their sin? What type of coat was it? The word indicates a long shirt like garment and would cover more than the aprons would. Were they both the same? When did the distinction of sexes in dress come into being? Here, or later? Ootsi the Ice Man - that ancient, preserved man discovered in the Alps, had on pants. Siberian cave paintings from ancient times, dated by secular researchers are far anterior to the Bibles dates, show men in pants and women in skirts and dresses. Interesting. And did God actually put it on them, or just provide it for them? The wording may indicate that God actually put it upon Adam and Eve. This could have implications for being clothed with God's righteousness. And were the coats still bloody?

Genesis 3:22 "And the LORD God said, 'Behold, the man is become as one of us, to know good and evil: and now, lest he put forth his hand, and take also of the tree of life, and eat, and live for ever:'"

Who was God speaking to here? The same beings as in 1:26? Himself? The context here definitely lends one to think the cherubim (vs. 24).

Whoever the "us" were, they knew good from evil. And fascinatingly enough, whatever the tree of life was, if man was to eat of it, he would live forever. Now the implication is clearly live forever, yet in a sinful decaying state worthy of eternal punishment. If man lived forever in sin, there could be no hope for the Sinless One, Jesus, to come and die for him. This propitiation was necessary for man to have the hope of Heaven. Maybe the way of the tree of life was not blocked to Lucifer and angels. So, they could eat, and there would be no sacrifice for them. But no, they have the second death as their future. So, the prohibition was an act of mercy by God, the disallowing of the fruit of the tree of life. Eat, and live forever in punishment by God. Or be forbidden it and partake of the fruit of the other tree of life, the cross, and be saved. If Adam was to live forever, then his offspring, Jesus according to the flesh, could not die. God in His mercy had a plan made for the latter. A close reading seems to indicate that this eating was a one-time eating, eat of the tree of life once, and live forever. But possibly not.

Going back to who God was speaking to, it appears God is speaking externally, and not to Himself. If God is three, there is no realistic way that He is a He. People say that man is three. Yes, but not three persons. One person in body, soul, and spirit.

Adam's descendants, if he would have been allowed by God to eat of the tree of life, would have lived under punishment forever. I am glad God stopped Adam from partaking. Adam and his descendants would have had what I imperfectly call sinful immortality. But God makes a way to the tree of life. 1 Door guarded by a flaming sword that turns every way. We will look more on that in a moment. And since Adam could still die, the last Adam could die as a substitution as well. The first Adam's death was senseless. The last Adam's death was salvic.

Genesis 3:23 "Therefore the LORD God sent him forth from the garden of Eden, to till the ground from whence he was taken."

So, God sends Adam and Eve West. If there was a tangible place of God's presence in the Garden, Adam must leave it. Jehovah Elohim, once again here used in Scripture, says Adam must go and till. No more garden of mercy, pleasure, and delights. No more free food.

Work was to be Adam's lot. And an intense bearing of children, hers. I'm assuming any offspring they may have had before the Fall was also cast out of the garden, as the penalty of sin, death, fell like a pall on all material kingdoms, plant and animal, that were under Adam's headship. Sorrow was their lot, not pleasure. God's mercy had been rejected, and punishment ensued. And not just for them, but for all living creatures, and the very earth itself. But God was still love.

It was said of Jesus, "And immediately the Spirit driveth him into the wilderness." Mark 1:12. Jesus was driven from the River Jordan into the wilderness. In verse 24 we see this sending of Adam was also described as the descriptive "drove." Just as Jesus the last Adam was driven into the wilderness, so the first man Adam is likewise driven into the wilderness of a fallen world, away from the tree of life and the former paradise of the garden. Just as the LORD God, Jehovah Elohim, (which usage many equate with a covenant Name of God), blessed man, now the full fruits of the curse come to bare. "For when we were in the flesh, the motions of sins, which were by the law, did work in our members to bring forth fruit unto death." decries Romans 7:5. Satan's fruit is always bitter. Since Adam was taken from the West to go to Eden, he is here sent back Westward. We have discussed at length why many think Adam was created somewhere in Israel.

Maybe there at his beginnings Adam would think and consider on what he had lost. He would be a link between paradise and curse. His voice along with Eve's would be a voice to progeny for the next 930 years. And as he toiled the dust from which he came, possibly he would ruminate on the consequences of his sin and use that as a warning to others. And start a revival. Genesis 4:26 "...then began men to call upon the name of the LORD."

Let us not forget God's grace even here in the midst of the Universe's most monumental tragedy. The soil had nutrients. The air was not totally corrupted. Man could breathe and live. The sun still shone. The stars still echoed their story. Man still had dominion. Animals would not overwhelm him. And God still loved mankind.

Out of the ground grew two trees, both of life, and knowledge of good and evil. It was not just the tree of knowledge, for Adam in the image of God had knowledge. But of good and evil. Other trees and plants came from the ground. And from the ground also came Adam.

The symbiosis of life is here seen. Adam, who came from the ground, was created to eat what came from the ground. He was created to chew, taste, digest, and have waste. All systems working in harmony. Speaking of which, I wonder if waste is a result of the Fall, or a part of man's original creation?

Genesis 3:24 "So he drove out the man; and he placed at the east of the garden of Eden Cherubims, and a flaming sword which turned every way, to keep the way of the tree of life."

This passage has much to unpack. It is very evident that the Garden had defined boundaries, with an entrance in the east. This is reminiscent of the Tabernacle and the Temple. The Church, the body of Christ likewise has boundaries. You are either in or out, in Christ or in Adam. In Christ are pleasures forevermore. In Adam, all is a desolate wilderness, where you have to work for sustenance. And it is possible to once be in the garden, and then remember what life was like after being driven out. And that driving out process could have been chilling. What was it like to not be able to go back? The driving out process would indicate that quite possibly man would turn around if he could. But he could not. Was life palpably different outside the garden, rather than within, yet fallen. I do not know.

Cherubim. We are here introduced to these unique beings. We have discussed them rather at length in regard to Genesis 1:26, 27. They had 4 faces, and hands as a man's. It is a proof of the Bible's veracity that most ancient cultures had a concept of Cherubim. You can see it in their artwork and sculptures. It is fascinating that evidently until the Flood, 1,648 years after this event that you could go and look at these Cherubim guarding the way of the tree of life evidently.

Cherubim were in the tapestry of the curtains and the veil of the tabernacle. Cherubim were on each end of the Ark of the Covenant (mercy seat). So, they are associated with man's approach unto God, and concealing God's glory. The Bible is likened to a flaming sword in Scripture (Jeremiah's fire and Hebrews 4 and Ephesians 6). Many put the flaming part as preaching. And there was only 1 way to the tree of life. The Bible shows us the way. Jesus is the way, the truth, and the life, no man can come unto the Father but by Him. So, what still guards the way of salvation, eternal life, is a sword (the Bible), and, as Scripture says, nothing is hid from the eyes of Him with whom we have to do. It turns every way and keeps that way sacrosanct. It pronounces Jesus to us. We do not know how many Cherubim were guarding the entrance, just that there were more than 1.

Lucifer is evidently a fallen cherub. Did other cherubs fall with him? Or just angels? We just do not know.

So, we began Chapter 3 with God placing man in the Garden. It ends with Him driving him out. God now places objects in man's way to prevent him from obtaining the tree of life.

Genesis Chapter 4
After Death Enters the World – Murder

GENESIS 4 SHOWS US what the fallen world will look like. And it looks very much like today. There is sibling rivalry, jealousy, murder, and then the origins of fallen civilization. It is a fascinating look. It is history. It would be impossible for myth makers to write this chapter. There are no supernatural legends, figures of superlative antiquity. It is rather a frank look at reality, the condition of mankind.

Verse 1 "And Adam knew Eve his wife; and she conceived, and bare Cain, and said, I have gotten a man from the LORD."

Life. Relationship. The first fallen child. Possibly Eve thought this was to be the seed to bruise satan's head. She would soon be sadly disappointed. He would rather bruise his brother in murder.

Even after sin, life goes on. Eve suffered the first consequence of her sin. The childbearing with sorrow. Adam and Eve, in the sweat of his brow, continued to obey God's command to be fruitful and multiply. Cain means "possession." I have lost the garden. I have gained Cain. We once again hear Eve speaking. And she credits the birth to Jehovah.

There are other things to explore here. "Knew" is a euphemism for intimacy. Therefore, many think the tree of knowledge of good and evil had to do with that subject. And modesty would once again come into play. Be that as it may, it is obvious Adam is the father of Cain from this verse, not the serpent. They were different kinds, Eve, and the serpent. Cohabitation would have been impossible. The language of the verse shows cause and effect. Adam knew Eve, and she conceived and bare Cain. Adam was the causal effect, not the serpent. Eve did not make love to the serpent at the Fall.

Might there be something deeper in Eve's words, though? If she understood the seed promise to be a virgin birth in 3:15, maybe she thought this was it, a man from the LORD. I have gotten a man from the LORD. But the verse, while allowing somewhat for this interpretation, does not demand it. It is far more probable the wonder of life is on Eve's lips here.

We find Adam did not divorce Eve. This concept did not yet exist in the natural world, I assume. All these things are for examples to us today. Adam and Eve would face the world's largest tragedy together. They did not fornicate. They did not do drugs or drink to our knowledge. They faced devastation together.

Also, we see she had a "man." The baby was called a man. Interesting.

Verse 2 "And she again bare his brother Abel. And Abel was a keeper of sheep, but Cain was a tiller of the ground."

It nowhere says at this time that Adam knew Eve to produce Abel. Therefore, some think Cain and Abel were twins. At the same time, just because Scripture does not record something, it does not mean it did not happen. So, Abel was the youngest, regardless. If they were twins that would possibly be a theme in Genesis. Zareh and Pharez, Jacob and Esau come to mind. Abel means "breath."

Abel kept sheep. If they were vegetarians, they would just use the by-product of sheep, such as the wool. Clothing again among other usages. And possibly for sacrifices, foretelling the Lamb of God that would take away the sin of the world. He that was slain from the foundation of the world. God created sheep for these purposes. Sheep also need mankind to care for them. Sheep are a proof of Creation.

Cain was a tiller of the ground. Just like dad, the firstborn followed in Adam's footsteps. Much has been made that Cain was bad, and this is exemplified by him tilling the cursed earth. But he had to eat. So, I see nothing necessarily nefarious with Cain tilling the ground. He could even feed Abel with the results of his tillage.

During the process of time that Cain and Abel became a farmer and a shepherd, surely more sons and daughters would have been born to Adam and Eve. Also, any offspring they had in the garden, which we would assume would have been driven out with them, would be in the world. These sources would be where Cain's wife came from, and also the people Cain was afraid of. Darrow tried to humiliate Bryan at the Scopes Trial with this question.

We see the beginnings of capitalism here. Abel would necessarily have to barter of the wool, the clothing, the tents, etc. made from the wool, in order to eat. Possibly even barter sheep for sacrifices to others. And Cain would have to use his excess surplus to purchase the material goods he needed. Rousseau longed for this day, and quite a bit of utopian literature in the 18th century looked at this as an ideal time. Alive before human government, people were just innately free.

4:3 "And in process of time it came to pass, that Cain brought of the fruit of the ground an offering unto the LORD."

We have no idea how long this process of time was. Long enough for other children to be born, grow and marry, seemingly. Ancient legend has it that Adam and Eve had 68 children if my memory serves me correctly, 41 sons and 27 daughters. In some traditions Cain's wife is Awan (Book of Jubilees). In others she is known as Jumelia. In these legends, her sister's name is Azura, who was married to both Abel, and later Seth. As far as when Cain and Abel were born, the text seems to indicate soon after the expulsion from the garden, so dates of 4004-2 BC would not be problematic.

Eridu in the ANE had the reputation of being the oldest city. Adapa was its first king. Adapa lost eternal life, it was said, by deception. Adam was taken to till the ground from whence he was taken, so it is unlikely he was here, since Eridu is a few hundred miles east of the Jerusalem area, unless he migrated back towards Eden over time. Possibly Adapa and the citizens of Eridu adopted the Genesis history as their own at a later time. It does appear that the LORD may have had a specific locale of worship. This may indicate Jerusalem, but it is very opaque on numerous levels. Possibly they could have offered wherever they pleased. The wording seems to favor Jehovah having a specific dwelling place. But what we do know is that Cain brought an offering of the ground to Jehovah.

How did Cain know to bring an offering to Jehovah? Probably he was told by Adam and Eve. Possibly he just intricately knew by the light of revelation. Maybe God had ordained it, and it just was not written. We really do not know. It is important to note that Cain did offer, however. He was not just an infidel from the beginning, so to speak. He at least went through the motions. But the motions of sin were at work in his body. Things were no longer perfect, including human nature.

Genesis 4:4 "And Abel, he also brought of the firstlings of his flock and of the fat thereof. And the LORD had respect unto Abel and to his offering:"

The difference of Cain and Abel's offerings were not just in substance, but in respect. Abel made sure that he brought of the firstlings and fat of his flock. The first fruits, so to speak. This is not mentioned regarding Cain's offering. But it was not just of the firstlings, but the fattest or best of the firstlings. Also, Cain brought an offering, indicating possibly just one, or a bare minimum. Abel, however brought firstlings, a plural amount. So, Abel's offering was better in quantity, in preference, and of quality. And since Abel respected God in this offering, God also respected him. And Abel's offering was better in these ways besides being a sheep instead of fruit from the cursed ground. The term "flock" indicates sheep, or something close.

I have deliberately brought views that I feel are sometimes overlooked in Chapters 3 and 4. God clothes Adam and Eve with a coat of skins. A blood sacrifice and the death of an animal. And here, Abel offers the blood of a lamb, while Cain offers of the cursed ground. And that is where most of the time the musings end. But if nothing is accidental or incidental in Scripture, God is trying to communicate something far more, as far as modesty and quality. This should not diminish blood sacrifice in any way, but rather give fullness to God's communication to man.

Man came from the ground. There seems to be type here. Man working to please God, instead of bringing God what God desires. God wants our best, not our leftovers. Bringing what we desire, rather than blood sacrifice which He desires, is not God's way. King Saul would later stumble and offer an imperfect sacrifice as well.

Genesis 4:5 "But unto Cain and to his offering he had not respect. And Cain was very wroth, and his countenance fell."

What was the sign Abel's offering pleased God while Cain's did not? Fire from heaven consuming the sacrifice? We are not told. But there was a tangible sign that told that Abel's offering was accepted while Cain's was not.

They must have been living near each other. Or possibly they came to sacrifice in the Presence of Jehovah at a certain time of year.

Cain was furious. Was he furious at God or Abel? Both? Was he aggrieved because of the labor he had to exert to bring forth this offering, the time it took to grow, and so forth? Did he think Abel had it easier? In reading the text, how it comes across is that Cain offered a perfunctory sacrifice, while Abel took care with his. And Cain's obligatory sacrifice was rejected while Abel's was respected. Jude verse 11 speaks of the way of Cain. Besides being a bloodless sacrifice, was his also just telling God take what I give you, not what You require? We should always give God our first and our best. Seek ye first the kingdom of God and His righteousness. The first fruits belong to the LORD. And as firstborn, maybe the ignominy of having to ask Abel for an appropriate sacrifice chaffed Cain.

Now Cain could have accepted the reproof of non-acceptance of his offering. He could have reassessed and asked how to please God? Cain certainly did not demonstrate repentance or remorse. But his anger was such he was wroth, and it affected his countenance. You could tell by looking at Cain that he was frustrated and upset. His inward emotions had crept outside.

Genesis 4:6 "And the LORD said unto Cain, Why art thou wroth? and why is thy countenance fallen?"

Here goes God asking questions again, questions that He already knows the answers to. God's purpose in doing this is to get us to confront our sins and shortcomings. For us to reason, consider, and think. And by so doing we can get back into right relationship with the Creator God of the Universe. Notice as well that God speaks to Cain, just as He did to Adam and Eve after they sinned. God speaking to us when we fail is an act of mercy and grace, and not a sign that all is well between us and Him.

So, God asks Cain, why are you wroth? And why has your countenance fallen? God is going to offer to Cain solutions to his problems in the next verse.

Genesis 4:7 "If thou doest well, shalt thou not be accepted? and if thou doest not well, sin lieth at the door. And unto thee shall be his desire, and thou shalt rule over him."

God asks Cain yet a 3rd question. I have nothing personal against you, God is telling Cain. If you do well, you will be accepted. The problem is not that I favor Abel over you. Rather, the issue is that Abel did well, so he was accepted. And you did not do well, so you were not accepted. It is fascinating that God does not just accept our crumbs or our leftovers. He wants our best. We must love Him with all our heart, soul, mind, and strength. This is a theme found throughout Scripture. In Malachi, some 3,500 years later we read that, "And if ye offer the blind for sacrifice, is it not evil? and if ye offer the lame and sick, is it not evil? offer it now unto thy governor; will he be pleased with thee, or accept thy person? saith the LORD of hosts."(1:8). God will not accept our leftovers. Like Saul's disobedience, majority obedience is still disobedience.

"Sin lieth at the door." What does that mean? This is one of the great disputed passages of Scriptural interpretation. Does it mean be careful Cain, you are about to sin? Or does it mean the sacrificial offering for sin is lying outside the door of your house? If it is the latter interpretation, it would mean that they lived in dwellings. And that quite possibly Cain and Abel lived in the same home, or very near one another. Over the decades, I have gone back and forth on the interpretation of this passage of Scripture. I am now well convinced that it is speaking of a sin offering. I will show how I came to that conclusion, and what the passage means if the 1st interpretation is correct.

God says the sin offering lies at the door. God in His mercy is offering a solution, not just confrontation. This sin is called a "his" here. So, it is either a metaphor, satan or a demon, or the sin offering. "…unto thee shall be his desire." That this is speaking of the sheep sin offering it seems clear. "And thou shalt rule over him" means the sheep is easily accessible. He will not run from you. You can get it, either at your brother's behest, or because Cain may have owned some sheep. Then you can bring it for an offering. If it is speaking of sin, how can man rule over him? Self-control? Discipline? This would seem to teach Pelagianism, that man does not have a sinful nature. I have friends who hold this view, of the Passage meaning sin and not a sin offering. I do not. The most natural reading to me is that the "his" refers naturally to the sin offering that Cain can graciously get. It is at his door. This is reminiscent of Christ the Lamb of God standing at the door and knocking. This also implicates that the blood sacrificial system, begun in 3:21, was continued. And this is how Noah knew to offer sacrifices to God after the Flood, as did Abraham. The innocent for the guilty. Substitution. Not everything is directly stated in Scripture. There are some things implicated.

So, we learn to this point from this episode that an average sacrifice will not do. A sacrifice of our choosing is not sufficient. We must offer our best, and what God requires. As we will see, this seems to sting Cain's pride. So, he kills the wrong thing.

Genesis 4:8 "And Cain talked with Abel his brother: and it came to pass, when they were in the field, that Cain rose up against Abel his brother, and slew him."

Cain talked with his brother. Had he decided to ask for a lamb? They were in the field, not the pasture. This may indicate they were on Cain's turf. Possibly the crops were high so they would be hidden. Whatever the case, Cain rises up against Abel, and slays him. Pride has, as a word, the connotation of being puffed or lifted up. Pride got the best of Cain. Only by pride cometh contention (Proverbs 13:10). Cain was not just contending with Abel, but with God. In 1 John 3:12 we get a great look of the situation here. It reads, "Not as Cain, who was of that wicked one, and slew his brother. And wherefore slew he him? Because his own works were evil, and his brother's righteous." The cause of murder was his wicked works. Cain's sacrifice was not just insufficient, it was wicked. Proverbs 21:27 also sheds light on this when it reads, "The sacrifice of the wicked is abomination: how much more, when he bringeth it with a wicked mind?" Cain, possibly the hope of the world in Eve's mind, is seen to be just a murderer. We have no idea how Adam and Eve must have felt. That is something for eternity.

Often times Cain is pictured slaying Abel with a rock. I see nowhere where the method is mentioned. It could have been a knife, his bare hands, or a rock. It is simply not recorded. "Rose up" could very well indicate some type of downward stroke. It does seem according to the New Testament ("NT" from here on out) that blood was shed, as well as in Gen. 4:10. Jesus, it is recorded twice, said Abel shed his blood in death (Matthew 23:35; Luke 11:51). And Hebrews 12:24 says, "And to Jesus the mediator of the new covenant, and to the blood of sprinkling, that speaketh better things than that of Abel." And Scripture says Abel offered his better sacrifice because of faith, showing faith was central to pleasing God even at this early period of mankind's history. In Hebrews 11:4 it reads, "By faith Abel offered unto God a more excellent sacrifice than Cain, by which he obtained witness that he was righteous, God testifying of his gifts: and by it he being dead yet speaketh."

This is the first recorded instance of murder in Scripture unless you include satan's murder of Adam and Eve (John 8:44). Maybe it is best to say this is the first recorded human against human murder. And it was brother against brother. Since the entire human race is related, all murder is really brother against brother, so to speak (or sister against sister, etc.). Abel had done correctly yet was killed. All who will live godly in Christ Jesus shall suffer persecution (2 Timothy 3:12).

Jealousy, pride, wrath, envy, hatred, rebellion. All these works of the flesh were resident in Cain, as they are in all of us. What type of child rearing did Adam and Eve use? How could 2 children raised by the same parents turn out so differently? It still happens today.

Genesis 4:9 "And the LORD said unto Cain, Where is Abel thy brother? And he said, I know not: Am I my brother's keeper?"

Man sins. God speaks. This seems counterintuitive that Holy God would speak to sinful man. The Word became flesh when man was lost, because God is good, not because man is good. But because man is bad, and in need of a Savior.

This dialogue is one of the most pathetic and pitiful found in Scripture. Cain's flippancy and arrogance bleed through the pages of Holy Writ. God again does as is customary. He asks a question He knows the answer to. He is wanting Cain to confront and confess his sin. Cain lies in all probability. How does he not know where Abel is? Unless someone came to bury him, or an animal drug him off, then Cain knows. And even if one of those things had occurred, Cain could still tell God. But he sneers. Am I my brother's keeper? Notice the word "keeper." In verse 2 it is noted that Abel is a keeper of sheep. So Cain, in one of the most petulance instances I am acquainted with anywhere, scorns at God, asking, Am I my brother's keeper? In debating the question whether we are our brother's keeper, we sometimes forget the mocking attitude it was first delivered in. It was total disrespect to God and Abel.

But are we our brother's keeper? In a sense, yes. But in a sense, everyone is responsible to work out their own salvation with fear and trembling. So, in that sense, no. But we should bear one another's burdens and so fulfill the law of Christ. Pray one for another. Rebuke and encourage one another. Fellowship with one another. But of course, there are limits.

We notice in Gen. 5:3 that Adam lived 130 years and begat Seth. If Seth were in the immediate aftermath of the death of Abel, Cain and Abel both could be over 100 years of age at this time. And if Adam and Eve kept obeying God to be fruitful and multiply during this time, the earth could have had quite a population. And that does not include any children Adam and Eve may have had before the Fall. There could easily have been 5 generations born, with each generation having children. And if the human DNA, and all DNA, was stronger in those days, being closer to perfection, quite a few children indeed could have been produced.

Genesis 4:10 "And he said, What hast thou done? the voice of thy brother's blood crieth unto me from the ground."

Again, we see God giving Cain an opportunity to tell the truth, to confess. The unmistakable characteristics of human nature are seen here. We have all felt the bite of guilt, the sting of shame, as a wrong is uncovered.

According to Hebrews 12:24, which perfectly confirms what is written here, Abel's blood spoke. It was crying to God from the ground. When these 2 verses are compared, it is evident that this is metaphorical. But it was speaking, nonetheless. The general consensus of what it was speaking was judgment. Man had been killed; blood had been shed. Judgement must come. Man is in the image of God. Just as satan was a murderer from the beginning and had killed Adam and Eve spiritually in immediacy and physically as the pains of death began to work in them, so now Cain is the murderer. There is a chance this is the first time blood had been shed besides sacrifice for sin. Now it was a symbol of man's pride. Jesus' blood cries mercy. So, Cain's charade is revealed. God rips his taunting arrogance in two. All is laid bare. And punishment is coming to Cain. Evidently the death penalty for shedding man's blood was not institutionalized until after the Flood in Genesis 9:6.

Genesis 4:11 "And now art thou cursed from the earth, which hath opened her mouth to receive thy brother's blood from thy hand;"

The earth had been cursed as God punished Adam. Now Cain, the tiller of the ground, is cursed from the earth. It is as if Abel's blood had poisoned the ground for Cain. Cain will no longer be a tiller of the ground. God will ensure that whatever he does in that regards shall not prosper. Sin separates. It separated Cain from his occupation. God metes out justice, well and justly. The blood was drunk by the earth. It symbolized death. Now the ground would be dead to Cain. We find this type of judgment from God repeatedly in Scripture, where He metes back what was done. Pharaoh had children killed in the Nile, so the Nile becomes blood. Israel missed 70 Sabbath years, so Israel must be in captivity 70 years. Nothing gets by the all-seeing eye of God. God is keeping score. But when God shed His own blood (Acts 20:28), it cried mercy. It brought life and deliverance.

There is another component here as well. Just as Cain would not humble himself to ask Abel for a sin offering, now he would have to humble himself to provide for himself and his family by asking, trading, or bartering. Just as keeping sheep can have a wandering component, now Cain must wander.

Genesis 4:12 "When thou tillest the ground, it shall not henceforth yield unto thee her strength; a fugitive and a vagabond shalt thou be in the earth."

Cain could try to till the ground, but it would be fruitless. When God opens, no man can shut. But when God shuts, no man can open. Since Cain would not be able to stay in one place for farming, he was to be a fugitive and a vagabond. A fugitive is one running from justice. He would be guilty until he died, so to speak. A vagabond is one that wanders from place to place, many times implying a degree of paupery. Cain go wherever you would like in the earth, but you will be guilty and wandering. Wandering like a sheep. Guilty like the sin offering. I wonder if he could have begun to raise sheep? Every shepherd is an abomination to the Egyptians (Genesis 46:34). It seems there is a parallel.

Earth is referred to here as "her." Mother earth may have allegorical beginnings very early in mankind's existence.

Genesis 4:13 "And Cain said unto the LORD, My punishment is greater than I can bear."

Cain goes from the scornful mocker to the victim. He killed Abel. But now his fugitive vagabond status is too much for him to bear. God's love and mercy is baked into the cake here. Cain deserved to die. He is merely getting punished. He got less than he deserved, but more than he expected. Sin always takes you further than you intended to go, keeps you longer than you intended to stay, and makes you pay more than you expected to pay.

Cain is not a good person. Yet Adam and Eve are here deprived of both of their sons. And they caused it. Cain must leave home.

Genesis 4:14 "Behold, thou hast driven me out this day from the face of the earth; and from thy face shall I be hid; and I shall be a fugitive and a vagabond in the earth; and it shall come to pass, that every one that findeth me shall slay me."

We have no record of Abel speaking, per se. Yet Cain continues to have his words recorded in Holy Writ. It hardly seems fair. But God is teaching us through the negative as well as the positive. Consider the ant (positive) and the sluggard (negative). Cain speaks 66 words in the Bible. The Bible also records the voice of satan, legion, Jezebel, and a host of other wicked people.

God drove Adam and Eve from the Garden. Here Cain says God drives him out from the face of the earth. Did Adam and Eve put the seed of this statement in him by recounting what had happened to them? We know not. But we do know Cain begins to complain. Complaining is a grievous sin in Scripture. And it basically began here in the human realm.

Observe as well that Cain said from God's face he would be hid. This is another indication that possibly there was a specific appointed place for worship. And Cain was saying he would no longer have access to it. Also notice that people would evidently be looking for Cain. Every one that findeth me shall slay me. A fugitive. And they shall kill me. It is totally lost on Cain that is what he deserved. He killed but being killed is too grievous a punishment for him.

I wonder if the earth was already so full of wickedness by this time, that since Cain would be divorced from his extended family, death would be his lot? That is a possibility.

Genesis 4:15 "And the LORD said unto him, Therefore whosoever slayeth Cain, vengeance shall be taken on him sevenfold. And the LORD set a mark upon Cain, lest any finding him should kill him."

God makes provision to preserve Cain's life to a large extent. God will exact vengeance on Cain's murder sevenfold. This would obviously discourage someone murdering Cain if this punishment were communicated through the Earth. How was this communicated throughout the earth? And what was this "magic" mark that was set upon Cain that would prevent his killing? We do not know the answer to any of these questions, but it had to be something obvious for everyone to know. I will not go into the various postulations of the mark of Cain, like Brigham Young's racist statement, but most really do not make sense. And the reason being they are not explanatory of how it could communicate to everyone not to kill Cain. What we do know is this seems to be God's love and mercy shining graciously on the scorning murderer Cain.

In Ezekiel, we have another instance of a mark being put upon certain people to prevent death. That is the similarity between this instance and Cain's situation. The differences are that the mark in Ezekiel was put upon the righteous as a designation. And those without the mark were slain evidently by an angel. Ezekiel 9:3, 4 gives a good backdrop. "And the glory of the God of Israel was gone up from the cherub, whereupon he was, to the threshold of the house. And he called to the man clothed with linen, which had the writer's inkhorn by his side;" (vs. 3). "And the LORD said unto him, Go through the midst of the city, through the midst of Jerusalem, and set a mark upon the foreheads of the men that sigh and that cry for all the abominations that be done in the midst thereof." (vs. 4). Also in the Book of Revelation the 13th chapter, no man may buy or sell unless they take a mark, or the name of the beast, or the number of his name, six hundred, three score, and six.

Adam and Eve were cursed. Now Cain is cursed. Both involved being driven out from God's presence. Instead of farming, Cain will be forbidden from farming. The remainder of this chapter is a fascinating and revealing look at the lineage of Cain.

Genesis 4:16 "And Cain went out from the presence of the LORD, and dwelt in the land of Nod, on the east of Eden."

So, Cain goes farther East than the Garden of Eden. "Nod" means "wandering." So, he went ostensibly from somewhere West of Eden, to now East of Eden. He was separated from Adam and Eve by the Garden. And he went out from the presence of the LORD. This is further evidence that there was a particular place where God's manifest presence dwelt, and this is where Cain and Abel brought their offerings. It certainly would not be out of place to say this was Jerusalem, but that is not definitely brought out in Scripture. But it could be implicated.

This land East of Eden seems to have been already named. There were evidently already wanderers in this area, indicating a multiplying of the population by this time. There could have been many thousands of people on the earth by now. Some who teach the creation of people in Genesis 1 is different from Adam and the Woman in Genesis 2 use this Scripture for evidence of their position. But as mentioned earlier, with 100+ years of procreation going on under far more idyllic circumstances, this view is certainly not necessitated.

Genesis 4:17 "And Cain knew his wife; and she conceived, and bare Enoch: and he builded a city, and called the name of the city, after the name of his son, Enoch."

Cain seems to have wanted his curse to stop with him. He built his son a city. A driven man in more ways than one. And this city's name was Enoch, which means "dedicated." Cain may wander, but he wanted his son to be free from wandering. But he named the city after Enoch. Adam named animals and Eve. Here Cain names a city. We can possibly get a hint that Cain's particular naming may pertain to wickedness when we read in John 5:43 these words, "I am come in my Father's name, and ye receive me not: if another shall come in his own name, him ye will receive." This is imperfect, I know, but possibly it is a gesture in that direction. John 5:43 is usually interpreted to be speaking of the antichrist. As far as the city goes, we don't know how large it was, what type buildings were in it, nothing really, other than the fact it was a city that Enoch, once he was grown, could settle into. Possibly Cain named it so all would know it belonged to his son.

Cain is cursed, he has sinned, yet he can still bear children. The goodness and mercy of God increases in our minds the deeper we look at Scripture.

Where did Cain get his wife, Clarence Darrow derisively asked an ailing William Jennings Bryan at the Scopes Monkey Trial. This Scripture is the first time we find out that Cain is married. His concern about his plight had been focused all about him. Notice Cain's wife did not divorce him. She followed. They had become one. At what time divorce entered the human conception we know not.

Genesis 4:18 "And unto Enoch was born Irad: and Irad begat Mehujael: and Mehujael begat Methusael: and Methusael begat Lamech."

Now we see Cain's lineage down to five generations. They were on the other side of the Garden, which quite possibly was a 100+ miles long. So, unless Adam and Eve travelled to see the offspring, or the offspring went back West to see them, they were separated from each other. Irad means "fleet." It is interesting to me how closely these names match up with even current designations for this area. The term "Irad" appears closely related etymologically to Iran and Iraq. Now whether there is an etymological connection, I am not sure of. It is fascinating, nonetheless even if it is a coincidental anomaly.

None of the wives' names are mentioned, including Cain's. This goes into the great unnamed women in Scripture category. And was

Abel married? We can assume since he would have probably been over 100, but the Scripture is silent. So that must not be a salient point in the eternal life narrative of the Bible.

Mehujael means "smitten by God." Part of Cain's curse, or a physical malady? Mehujael also looks much like a modern Middle Eastern name. The Ja and El at the end of his name seem to be for Jehovah and Elohim. Methusael means "who is God," God being seen in the "El" at the end of his name. This name could mean anything from not knowing God because he was not in the presence of God towards the West, to a scorning of God like his heritage. Lamech means "powerful." Again, is this a sign of pride in Cain's genealogies? Many associate not just Cain, but his lineage with evil. Lamech, being powerful, would later kill a man like Cain did. Names throughout Scripture play a significant role.

Genesis 4:19 "And Lamech took unto him two wives: the name of the one was Adah, and the name of the other Zillah."

This is the first mention of polygamy in the Bible. This further buttresses the speculation that Cain's lineage was evil. It goes against God's original intent in Scripture. If they all dwelt near the city of Enoch, they did not have the teaching of Adam and Eve possibly and were continually separated from God's Presence. Maybe Cain taught his children not to serve God. But these are just possibilities, not absolutes set in stone. Maybe they could see the Cherubim and the flaming sword guarding the entrance to the Garden.

Observe that Lamech took him 2 wives. The man initiated the marriage. Also notice he committed himself to them, and they to him. They are called wives, so it seems a marriage covenant was established. Adah means "ornament." Possibly she was very beautiful. Or maybe she began to wear jewelry. Zillah means "shade." It could be she was tall, among other interpretations. Or maybe her parents just wanted relief from the Middle Eastern heat. We do not know anything of the lineage of Adah or Zillah. We are not told how long Cain lived. It must not be important. There are many other things that are listed and known; hence God sees them as important to us.

Genesis 4:20 "And Adah bare Jabal: he was the father of such as dwell in tents, and of such as have cattle."

Now we come to the sixth generation from Cain, and the seventh generation from Adam. Jabal seems to have picked up his lifestyle from Cain, in a sense. He was possibly the first nomad or Bedouin. Cain wandered. Jabal seems to have made it a profitable lifestyle. Jabal means "stream of water," which, of course, fits a nomadic lifestyle. It does seem names were almost given prophetically at birth, that what a person was named became a big part of who they were. This may go back to a correlative with Adam naming animals in the garden, and naming Eve after the Fall based on her attribute of being the mother of all living.

The powerful (Lamech) and the ornament (Adah) give birth to the dweller in tents and those that have cattle. If man were still not a meat eater, I would assume the cattle were for milk, and their hides for various uses. And as cattle in Scripture is a generic term for domesticated animal, other uses could be found as well.

On a side note, since ancient man was brilliant, I wonder what this city of Enoch looked like? And I wonder if there were other cities? And other places named like the land of Nod was? If the cities were anything like the immediate post flood cities, they were probably more opulent and more enduring than anything we are building now. Archaeology is a neglected discipline in so much of the popular world and gives great insight into early man.

Genesis 4:21 "And his brother's name was Jubal: he was the father of all such as handle the harp and organ."

Jubilee. What a word. Indicative of festivity and music. Jubal, the father, or the first, was the originator of all who would handle the harp and the organ. So, Adah and Lamech once again bare a child, and he invents musical instruments. Now where was satan and the demons this entire time? I am assuming going to and fro and doing what they always do. Since satan seems to have been a musical instrument, did he have a hand in this? Or since man is in the image of God, was it something inherent in man to invent? Jubal and Jabal, being so close etymologically, could have been twins, but that is by no means definite. Jubilee would come to mean releasing from debt and captivity to Israel. That this concept correlated with music is quite interesting.

When David was playing his harp, he had this knowledge from Jubal millennia before. When Asaph and Jeduthun played, sang, wrote, and prophesied through music, it went back to Jubal. I guess this knowledge of instruments went with Noah's family through the Flood. On a side note, it is mentioned in Scripture that David invented musical instruments in Amos 6:5. People are still inventing them today.

Genesis 4:22 "And Zillah, she also bare Tubalcain, an instructer of every artificer in brass and iron: and the sister of Tubalcain was Naamah."

Lamech's other wife, Zillah, bare Tubalcain, which means "thou wilt be brought of Cain." Possibly this means Cain was still alive at his birth. Jubal and Jabal were known as fathers, or beginners of. Tubalcain was an instructor. He taught people how to work with brass and iron. Certainly, the earliest cities of the Ancient Near East bare testament to the incredible metallurgical skill they possessed.

Naamah means "loveliness." There are so many types of loveliness. It is so multifaceted. So, to recap, Cain's offspring gives us cities, music, nomads, husbandry, polygamy, and metallurgy.

Genesis 4:23 "And Lamech said unto his wives, Adah and Zillah, Hear my voice; ye wives of Lamech, hearken unto my speech: for I have slain a man to my wounding, and a young man to my hurt."

Lamech got into a fight. We do not know with who or why. This was not like Cain, where Abel, as a type of Christ possibly, and it is not recorded that he fought back. This was something that even though Lamech won the fight, he was wounded and hurt. Lamech killed just as surely as Cain did, but the circumstances remain vague.

"Hear my voice." This plays a large role in Genesis, and throughout Scripture. "God said" is repeated in Genesis 1 numerous times. God speaks to Adam in Chapter 2. The serpent speaks in Chapter 3, then the Voice of the LORD walks in the Garden. Cain and God dialogue earlier in Chapter 4. Lamech here seems to be venting to his wives. He says "hearken unto my speech" for emphasis. Maybe this is the beginning of the Hebrew Hendiadys, which is a Jewish repetition of thought. You see this often in Scripture.

God did not ordain polygamy. Adam and Eve is the standard and the archetype for marriage.

Genesis 4:24 "If Cain shall be avenged sevenfold, truly Lamech seventy and sevenfold."

The phraseology here seems unmistakable. Cain seems to still be alive. This is certainly not surprising with lifespans of 900+ years common before the Flood. Lamech seems to be pushing into an arrogant mold. God pronounced the punishment of sevenfold on those that would kill Cain. But here is Lamech doing the pronouncing. And it is not just sevenfold, but 70 and sevenfold. This is just pure, unbridled arrogance, and an attempt to get out of punishment. God in His mercy gave Cain that grace of severe punishment if one would try to kill him. Lamech's is a declaration of defiance.

Genesis 4:25 "And Adam knew his wife again; and she bare a son, and called his name Seth: For God, said she, hath appointed me another seed instead of Abel, whom Cain slew."

The disappointment of Eve in Cain's murder of Abel. They would not be the seed that bruises the head of the serpent. It was also none of Adam and Eve's other unnamed offspring. Could hope be found in Seth? Seth means "compensation." Seth was a replacement for Abel. Since Cain was alive yet wandering, he needed no replacement. Eve faces reality. She acknowledges that Cain has murdered her son. The naming of children seems to alternately be either by the husband or wife at this point in Scripture. We hear Eve speak yet again. Naming a son and acknowledging the goodness of God. Fascinatingly it is not just Adam that can name as in Genesis 2 and 3. Eve also here speaks fondly of Elohim. And the use of the words "appointed," and "seed" hearken back to 3:15. We find in Luke 3 that Seth is in the line of the Messiah, but of course, not the Messiah.

Each time Eve would bear a child, the pain and longevity of gestation must have brought her mind back to what she had lost in Eden. If only she had not listened to the serpent. Adam and Eve were the two that had been in a perfect world, and now lived in the world of sorrow and woe. From wow to woe, so to speak. They were a bridge of what was, to what is. People, including Cain and his lineage, could go to the entrance of paradise. But Cherubim and a flaming sword guarded the entrance.

On a practical note, it is good to be patient. God many times will replace what we have lost. Remember the patience of Job.

Genesis 4:26 "And to Seth, to him also there was born a son; and he called his name Enos: then began men to call upon the name of the LORD."

We have left the line of Cain. We move to the Sethite line. According to Genesis 5:6, 105 years elapse between 4:25 and 26. Seth was 105 years old when Enos was born. Adam would have been 235 years old. Some say 265, because they are assuming that Adam was created a 30-year-old man in the Garden. I would like to know if there is proof of that other than speculation. Even though Adam had the appearance of age, and created fully grown, chronologically he was still zero-one when created, not 30. This particular verse 26, would have been in 3769 BC according to Ussher.

We also need to keep in mind as we go through the line of Seth, that it was congruent with the line of Cain. The dates for the Cainite line are not given but are for the Sethite line. They must be significant for God to want us to know them.

Enos means "man," or "mortal man." Some say it means "vanity" or even "misery." Man, or mortal man will suffice as being very accurate. Enos uniquely enough is given great currency in Islam. He is mentioned as a prophet, and in the genealogy of Muhammed.

The last part of verse 26 is one of the most controversial in all of Scripture. There are many that say the Hebrew conclusively means that men began to call themselves Jehovah, and not in a submissive sense. They were claiming to be God. They were claiming the promise of the serpent in Genesis 3:5. Others may take a slightly different tack and say that men began to use the name of Jehovah (LORD) in vain. To me, the verse seems to indicate revival. Eve credited God with another seed. Now another blessing comes. And people began to call upon the name of the LORD. In the New Testament, this phraseology has connotations of Jesus' Name baptism. Possibly it is a gesture towards that. Calling upon the Name of the LORD will be a theme throughout Scripture.

2 Chronicles 7:14 "If my people, which are called by my name, shall humble themselves, and pray, and seek my face, and turn from their wicked ways; then will I hear from heaven, and will forgive their sin, and will heal their land."

Acts 2:21 "And it shall come to pass, that whosoever shall call on the name of the Lord shall be saved." Theologians would say this indicates Jesus' Name baptism.

Zephaniah 3:9 "For then will I turn to the people a pure language, that they may all call upon the name of the LORD, to serve him with one consent." And quite possibly that pure language will be whatever language was being spoken here. With Dr. Douglas Petrovich discovering that Joseph, Ephraim, and Manasseh created the first consonantal alphabet from Hieroglyphics, and that language was (Paleo) Hebrew, it brings more fascinating research to the subject. I realize this is 2,000 years after the fact, but quite possibly it was Hebrew being spoken here. If the Bible is forever settled in Heaven, it obviously was written in some language.

Chapter 5

Genesis 5 is primarily about the Godly Sethite line. We are also introduced to well-known Bible characters such as Methuselah, Enoch, and Noah with his sons. Biblical chronology also plays an important role here, as we see that mankind lived far longer before the Flood than afterwards.

Genesis 5:1 "This is the book of the generations of Adam. In the day that God created man, in the likeness of God made he him;"

This is the second usage of the term "generations" in Genesis. It is the first time the word "book" is used. That is the reason many feel this was a scroll or clay tablet that was handed down until Moses' day, going with Noah's family on the ark. Possibly, but not necessarily. We know this time period had a high culture. It was very learned. So, they could have written by various means. It could be Moses saying this as he wrote the Pentateuch. But we know it was a book, whatever the particular meaning. And the writing could obviously have been done in the antediluvian period.

It is here reiterated that God made man in one day, and that man was in the likeness of God. We also see that Adam and man are synonymous in the beginning. This is an important point for those that feel Genesis 1 and 2 were different creations of men. Also, here are some things to consider when looking through the genealogies of Scripture. First, they must be important for God to include them. Ages and lengths of day are likewise important when God chooses to include that information. Try and consider the centuries that passed when they are presented to us in just one or two sentences. And see if there are any incidental messages that God is trying to teach us.

Chronologies are considered by most to be the most boring parts of Scripture, but they do not have to be. I have found that the more I read the Bible, the more the genealogies stand out. One last thing. The meaning of the names in Scripture can many times play a vivid role of what God is trying to communicate. But do not go overboard with it.

Genesis 5:2 "Male and female created he them; and blessed them, and called their name Adam, in the day when they were created."

This is where the tradition comes for the woman to take the man's name in marriage, though this is not always followed in Scripture. In that same day, God created male and female. There are only two genders. Even with genetics breaking down because of slight mutations from generation to generation, there are still only two genders. Even those born with certain malformities have only one gender or the other overwhelmingly in their DNA.

Notice Male and Female did not evolve. God created them. He did not create them through evolutionary processes. He did not infuse preexisting hominids with souls. They were special creations of God, in His image and in His likeness.

The first thing God did with mankind was to bless them. He has not only benevolent intentions toward us, but blessed and favorable intentions toward us. We and satan are the author of any bad things that occur to us. This blessing by God extends until today. Our bodies are still alive with procreation, and in each person is the potential to fill many universes with offspring (Not in a Mormon sense). This is the grace of life.

Again, it is reemphasized that Adam and Eve were created in one day. "Day" occasionally means "time-period," but depending on its context, it most times refers to a literal 24-hour day consisting of day and night.

Eve was not named "Eve" until after the Fall. I mistakenly often call her Eve before that point. But in reality, she is the Woman, and any name she had would fall under the auspices of Adam. That portion of Genesis 2 is sometimes referred to as the first wedding ceremony. The Bride is brought to the Groom. She takes his name. Procreation begins. Just as we are the bride of Christ. It is important to take His Name in water baptism. And He infills us with His Spirit.

Genesis 5:3 "And Adam lived an hundred and thirty years, and begat a son in his own likeness, after his image; and called his name Seth:"

This is an expansion of 4:25. Cain, Abel, and other children that were born in-between their birth and Abel's death are not mentioned. He lived 130 years, and begat Seth. We were briefly introduced to Seth in the previous chapter, and his son Enos.

What did Adam do for 130 years? Till land and raise children. Eve raised and bore children. The phrase "in his own likeness, after his image" is significant. Everything reproduces after its kind. Just as God reproduced after His image in Adam, so here Adam reproduces after his image in Seth. All this likely looks toward the great event when God would become a Man in Christ Jesus. All things were created by this event. Jesus was the Lamb slain from the foundation of the world. So, Adam was created in God's image. Are we still in God's image? Yes, but fallen. In 4:25 it appears that Eve named Seth, while here it is said that Adam did. They must have worked together on the name, or else what one does can be attributed to the other since they are one flesh.

Being so near the Fall, man's DNA must have been stronger. Having children at 130 and well beyond was commonplace. Statisticians tell us after examining this portion of Scripture, that by the time the Flood hit, seven billion plus people could have easily been on planet earth. This is also another proof of a young earth. If the earth's population had been growing for 10,000s of thousands of years, there would not be enough room in the solar system to fit everyone.

I do want to stress before moving on to verse 4 that calling, and naming things plays a large part of Biblical theology from earliest creation through the New Birth experience we have today.

Genesis 5:4 "And the days of Adam after he had begotten Seth were eight hundred years: and he begat sons and daughters:"

So, Adam continued to be blessed, and continued to obey God in begetting sons and daughters. What was it like as Adam grew older? What were his memories of paradise and the Fall like? What was it like to see the world go from unpopulated to far more populated? How did the trees look different after the Fall? Animals? The sky?

Adam and Eve never divorced. They were never unfaithful to one another as far as we know. When was the first divorce? The first unfaithfulness? We know when the first polygamy was, so possibly that counts as the first unfaithfulness. Eve messed up. But it was not fornication, especially not with the serpent, which would have been cause for divorce.

Genesis 5:5 "And all the days that Adam lived were nine hundred and thirty years: and he died."

The first man died. Crowned Adam perished. Ussher gives the year as 3074 BC. I have no reason to dispute that. Ussher was meticulous in his research. Read him sometime. Seth would have been 800, and Methuselah would have been 243 at Adam's death. This is significant. Methuselah lived until the Flood came. So, from Paradise to the Flood, at least one person, and possibly an untold multitude more, overlapped Adam significantly. In Methuselah's case 243 years.

Enoch, Cainan, Jared, Mahalaleel, Enos, and probably all of Cain's line mentioned in Chapter 4, lived contemporaneously with Adam, as well as the unnamed sons and daughters mentioned as having been born throughout this genealogy.

We do not know how Adam died. The Bible is stunning in its simplicity. "And he died" is all we know. We see no regalness. We know of no exquisite funeral. We simply know he died. We know not when Eve passed. We are not even sure if Adam was saved, though through the opaqueness we see glimmers that he was.

What a difference a sin makes. From eternal bliss and love, to death and sin for all. The differences between the promises of God, and sin with its terrible ramifications of death, suffering frailty, and humility, are accounted for with one sin. One act of terrible disobedience. And the Divine justice of the Universe and beyond begins. 930 years old seems ancient to us. But it was a drop in the bucket of the blessings God had intended for us, with eternal pleasure. The last verse of Genesis, the Book which begins crowned with glory, haunts us. The last words of Genesis are "…a coffin in Egypt."

All the days of Adam. What were they like? Farming, sweating, toiling, hurting, thinking, raising children. Did he blame Eve for suffering and death? What were his thoughts? How often did he think of Paradise? Was he saved? Evidence indicates he might have been. The Bible says, "As he spake by the mouth of his holy prophets, which have been since the world began:" Luke 1:70. See also Acts 3:21 and Luke 11:50. Adam was a prophet. He prophesied that a man would leave his father and mother and cleave to his wife, and they would be one flesh. Luke 13:28 says all the prophets will be saved ("There shall be weeping and gnashing of teeth, when ye shall see Abraham, and Isaac, and Jacob, and all the prophets, in the kingdom of God, and you yourselves throughst out."). Of course, this excludes false prophets. So scripturally it appears Adam was saved. And he died.

We find references to Adam scattered throughout the New Testament. You cannot dispute the Genesis account of the original Adam without damaging the remainder of Scripture. In Romans 5 he is presented as the head of creation, the federal head as theologians define it. And when he sinned, repercussions were loosed upon God's creation in the form of death, decay, and suffering. Was Adam aware of God's plan from the foundation of the world, that God would become a Man and save us? Or did he live rather hopeless, with Genesis 3:15 as a distant dream of deliverance? Adapa, the Mesopotamian reference it seems to Adam, had died. He lived long according to our standards, but not in the fullness he could have.

Genesis 5:6 "And Seth lived an hundred and five years, and begat Enos:"

Genesis 4:26 is here fleshed out. This would have been around 3769 BC. Adam would have been around 235 years old according to Ussher. The assumption is that the genealogies mentioned here are qualified firstborns. Cain was cursed and Adam was dead. Now Seth brings forth. Hebrews 7:9, and 10 shares an interesting point concerning procreation. It reads thusly, "And as I may so say, Levi also, who receiveth tithes, payed tithes in Abraham. For he was yet in the loins of his father, when Melchisedec met him." Levi was considered alive in Abraham, though Abraham was his great-grandfather, and died well before Levi was born (Abraham died about 1821 BC, and Levi was born around 1755 BC). So, the reason we are born tainted in sin is because we were alive in Adam, and when he sinned, we sinned, so to speak, or at least got the corruption of death passed down to us. At this time, when Enos was born, people began to call on the name of Jehovah. Revival broke out. There was a Cainite lineage, sure. But there was also a line that wanted Jehovah. That dynamic tension seems to be throughout history to greater and lesser degrees.

1 Chronicles 1 opens with these genealogies. Luke 3 ends with them. Man survives and earth abides.

Genesis 5:7 "And Seth lived after he begat Enos eight hundred and seven years, and begat sons and daughters:"

Seth lived until 2962 BC. Enos would have been 807 at this time. Seth would have been alive to see his father Adam die in 3074 BC, some 112 years before his own death. The Hebrew calendar begins soon after the birth of Enos, in 3761 BC. We will not take the time to look at calendar discrepancies. Seth would have been alive through the Cainite genealogy of Chapter 4, and through Enoch's translation in 3017 BC. He would have missed the birth of Noah by 14 years. As fascinating as it would be to have a detailed look at the life of these earliest of Patriarch's, that was not God's intention. And as interesting as a fictional novel would be of this time-period, it would be just that-

fiction. Suppositions could be made concerning language, culture, living conditions and the like, but no real independent verification could be forthcoming, until that great resurrection day.

We have no way of knowing how many sons and daughters Seth had. But if he were being fruitful and multiplying, the earth could have quickly been expanding in population. And uniquely enough, the wives are largely unmentioned throughout Chapter 5. Again, silence should not be mistaken for unimportance, as procreation could not have occurred without the spouse. And if the population of the earth was really approaching 7 billion or more before the Flood, there is a limited number of names that could be mentioned in this genealogy. So, the slight of the wives' names is ameliorated. The focal point of Scripture is Jesus. There are many incidental items which are left unsaid. The Bible is expansive in its chronology but limited in its details.

Mankind must have been exceedingly brilliant. Living to such long ages, knowledge surely increased. Yet the moral predicament of mankind led to destruction, not human improvement. What a folly for us to think we can usher in a utopia on earth. Sinful human nature, as well as satanic forces block our path.

Genesis 5:8 "And all the days of Seth were nine hundred and twelve years: and he died.

In 2962 Seth died. He overlapped Adam by 800 years. The tie with perfection was still there. Adam and Eve could communicate of life in the Garden. Seth could see the entrance blocked by the flaming sword and the Cherubim if he so desired. This oral tradition must have been strong, but possibly not encompassing. With so many being born, the population of earth would grow scattered and the message of creation would weaken.

Another lesson to contemplate is the use of the word "days" here. Not years. It is as if God was wanting us to number our days. It is one thing to count years, decades, centuries, and the like. Even weeks and months. But we do not live in those. We live in days. And each day makes a life. Do not waste time, said Ben Franklin, for that is the stuff that life is made of. Take no thought of the morrow, Jesus said, for sufficient unto the day is the evil thereof. Seth lived days. Ups and downs, happiness and sorrow, contemplation, and work. Raising a family along with alone time. We do not know Seth's occupation, per se by the way, but farming would be a guess. Maybe a shepherd like Abel. But it is not mentioned. How close did he live to Adam and Eve? To his sons and daughters? To Adam and Eve's sons and daughters? The family of Cain? Interesting to think about, impossible to know outside of Divine revelation.

Was Seth saved? I have no idea. If this is the Godly Sethite line, then yes. But Scripture gives no definitive answer. To the extreme Bible literalist, Seth died the day he turned 912. I am 53 as I write this. But I do not say I am 53 and so many days. The same goes here. Some things are not given in Holy Writ.

Here in the fifth chapter of Genesis in the Bible the word death is repeated over and over. It began in Chapter 3. And that fateful appointment is for all mankind.

Genesis 5:9 "And Enos lived ninety years, and begat Cainan:"

This occurred in 3679 BC. Cainan is the equivalent of Kenan (1 Chronicles 1:2) and means "possession." What happened during these 90 years, the training Enos received, his marriage, the sunsets, feelings, smells, sights, and emotions, we know not.

Genesis 5:10 "And Enos lived after he begat Cainan eight hundred and fifteen years, and begat sons and daughters:"

Once again it is shown that he obeyed the command to be fruitful and multiply. Entropy had not blunted the genetic stream. We have no idea who these sons and daughters were. They will be revealed in eternity. The Bible is sublime in its compactness and expansiveness.

When Cainan was born, Adam would have been 325 years of age. His grandfather Seth about 195.

Genesis 5:11 "And all the days of Enos were nine hundred and five years: and he died."

His death is presumed to be of old age. The succinctness of the phrase is sudden. Adam lived to be 930, Seth 912. They died. Enos would have lived until about 2864 BC. Noah would have been about 84 at the time of his death. His life would have coincided with the translation of Enoch in 3017 BC. Seth's would have as well. The Book of Jasher presents Enoch as an isolated King, watching the world descend into wickedness. There are different iterations of the Book of Jasher, and I am not sure that any that we currently possess are what was referred to in Holy Writ, in whole or in part. And be that as it may, even if it was that referenced in Scripture, since it is not included in the Canon of Scripture, we could not vouch for its veracity in all points. Possibly Seth, Enoch, Adam, and Enos had sweet fellowship together, but that is unknowable on this side of Glory. Eight times in Chapter 5 these nine letters, three words with three syllables communicate the awful spectre that Adam introduced into the world, "and he died." In seeming continuation with the narrative, the next time we find this phrase is in reference to Noah in Genesis 9:29. It is first found in Chapter Five.

Genesis 5:12 "And Cainan lived seventy years, and begat Mahalaleel:"

There are many great books on the significance of numbers in Scripture. Ed Vallowe has one, as does Ethelbert William Bullinger. John J. Davis does as well. And since there is nothing accidental or incidental in the Bible, there is significance. The Jews call it Gematria. And here we come to the number 70. Jesus sent out 70 in Luke 10. There are 70 weeks appointed on Israel in Daniel 9. The punishment of Jerusalem in Daniel's time was 70 years. Terah was 70 when he begat Abram, Nahor, and Haran. 70 souls came with Jacob to Egypt (Exodus 1:5). 70 elders went with Moses and Aaron to the mount. 70 elders were with Moses in Numbers 11. Gideon had 70 children as did Ahab. Tyre was forgotten 70 years.

70 elders worshipped the sun in Ezekiel's day in Ezekiel Chapter 8. Jesus said to forgive 70 times 7 in trespasses of a brother. So there seems to be some significance here. Numbers around 70 occur far less frequently in Scripture, if at all. What 70 indicates should be fleshed out at another time, God willing. The number 70 occurs 61 times in 60 verses in the KJV.

Mahaleel means "praise of God," so it is likely Cainan praised God at the birth of his son. Maybe they had a copy of Scripture and knew that was to be his name. This gives indication that this is a Godly line, with praise to the Almighty. A fascinating thing about the genealogies here is that everyone on earth can trace their lineage back to them, through Noah. Another interesting thing to note is that the ages of the evident firstborn that was begotten continues to get younger to this point. Adam was 130 with Seth, though Seth was not the firstborn. Seth was 105. Enos was 90. Cainan was 70, and we will see that Mahaleel was 65.

Then the cycle of getting younger with each proceeding generation stops. And again, the assumption is that these are all firstborns, but I am not sure that the Scripture says that or demands it. It might, but I cannot think of a particular reference at the moment.

Genesis 5:13 "And Cainan lived after he begat Mahalaleel eight hundred and forty years, and begat sons and daughters:"

Mahalaleel would have been born around 3609 BC. The phraseology seems to indicate that Cainan and the others begat sons and daughters until they died. Going back to the significance of the number 70, Cainan lived 840 years after he begat Mahalaleel, which is 70 times 12. He lived until he was 910, which is 70 times 13.

After the Flood, this same line would have women who had difficulty in childbearing in Sarai, Rebekah, and Rachel. But not now. The Genetics were still too close to Eden.

Genesis 5:14 "And all the days of Cainan were nine hundred and ten years: and he died."

His death according to Ussher's excellent genealogy would have been about 2769 BC. He would have been contemporary with Adam for 605 years, Enoch for 365 years, Noah for 231 years, Methuselah for 603 years, and Seth for 717 years. Noah lived after the Flood about 350 years, or until 1998 BC, approximately. So here we have someone who would have been contemporaneous with Adam and the remembrances of the perfect world for 605 years, while simultaneously contemporary with Noah who lived 3.5 centuries after the Flood, and into the 2nd millennium BC. So much information could have been transmitted, even without a written Scripture during this time. Also, for perspective, he would have died much closer to the Flood than the Fall - the two great judgments of man's first 1656 years of existence. We have had it relatively easy since. Just joking, because the Fall is still in effect.

Genesis 5:15 "And Mahalaleel lived sixty and five years, and begat Jared:"

Jared is a name that is still in use quite frequently in the USA. It means "descent" or "descendant." If only Darwin could have seen the descent of man from the state of perfection until now. The Pseudepigraphal book of Jubilees suggest that Jared's name of "descent" referred to the angels that descended in his days and began to intermarry and impregnate women. The fact that angels did this has long been a part of Jewish theology. Conservative Jews also by and large ascribe to serpent seed theory, and Pelagianism as well (man has no sinful nature).

Jared would have been born about 3544 BC or 460 years Anno Mundi (after the creation).

Genesis 5:16 "And Mahalaleel lived after he begat Jared eight hundred and thirty years, and begat sons and daughters:"

This 4th from Adam, or his Great-great grandson continued to live and begat. The only early exceptions we see to this in this line are Abel and Enoch. In Cain's line, the man who Lamech killed did not live out his full earthly life, though the deceased himself was not necessarily of Cain's lineage.

Genesis 5:17 "And all the days of Mahalaleel were eight hundred ninety and five years: and he died."

Mahalaleel lived to be 895. Adam lived to 930, Seth 912, Enos 905, and Cainan 910. So, in this particular genealogy Mahalaleel is the first to die before 900 years of age. This may indicate a weakening of the DNA, and/or an increase in pathogens. Mahalaleel died in 2714 BC, and Jared would have been 830. The burial practices, or the disposing of corpses of these ancient Patriarchs would be interesting to know.

Genesis 5:18 "And Jared lived an hundred sixty and two years, and he begat Enoch:"

"Praise," "descent," "dedicated." That is the meaning of the names of the three last Patriarchs mentioned. "Possession," "vanity" and "despair," "replacement," and "man" would have been the others before that. Enoch lights upon the scene like a thunderbolt. This Enoch, "dedicated," is mentioned nine times in nine Scriptures, including thrice in the NT, in contradistinction to the Enoch, offspring of Cain, mentioned in Chapter 4. The lack of chronology in the Cainite chronology, I will mention again, is telling. It is also to be noted that Jared was the oldest mentioned to this point before begetting a child. Of course, the many millions who would have been populating the earth at this time are not listed, so we have no way of knowing specifics with them. Since the theme of Scripture is Jesus, only His genealogy appears specifically relevant in Holy Writ. The birth of Enoch would have been somewhere around 3382 BC, and Adam would have been 622. We have no way of knowing if Adam and Enoch ever spoke, or if they were dwelling in close proximity to one another. It would be interesting to know if people made pilgrimages to speak with Adam and Eve. Or did Adam and Eve go on a speaking circuit? Or did they live a life of relative obscurity? Most probably they could not travel far because of agricultural obligations. It is at least possible that this entire family structure lived within close proximity, but we don't know this for sure. If all these Patriarchs continued to have children until they died, it appears their wives possibly outlived them. Or when they died, and He called their name Adam in Genesis 5:2, did they die simultaneously since they were 1 flesh? It is possible, but again, we have no way of knowing. I highly doubt it. In some cultures, even still, the wife is required to die with the husband, but this is denounced rightly as archaic barbarism.

Seth would have been 492 at Enoch's birth, Enos 387, Cainan 297, Mahalaleel 227, and, of course, Jared 162. I put this information in here to try and give us a context of what was happening in the world at this time. It is many times easy to get lost in verse, so to speak, reading of living, giving birth, having more children, and then death, and not adequately recognizing there are overlapping lives. It seems difficult to assimilate this in reading the Sacred Text.

Genesis 5:19 "And Jared lived after he begat Enoch eight hundred years, and begat sons and daughters:"

Jared is mentioned in the Qu'ran. In Jubilees it is said he married a woman named Bereka, and his mother's name was Dinah in this pseudepigraphal book. In the fallacious Samaritan Pentateuch, Enoch was born when he was 62 and he died at 847. All of this is mentioned as information, and its veracity of course is highly doubtful.

Now Jubilees is a book that was known to the Dead Sea Scroll community and is considered to be part of the canon by the Ethiopian Orthodox Church and Ethiopian Jews. It is also known as Lesser Genesis, or lepto-genesis, and contains 50 chapters. It dates from the mid-2nd century BC according to most. It is not considered authoritative or accurate.

Genesis 5:20 "And all the days of Jared were nine hundred sixty and two years: and he died."

To this point, Jared is the oldest living human recorded. Of course, the record is very limited, considering the probable billions that lived between the Fall and the Flood. Jared's death would have been about 2582, or 234 years before the Deluge.

In Scripture, it is not recorded anyone lived to reach the millennium mark, 1,000 years of age. The day equals a thousand-year hypothesis is given as the reason why by some. While this is possible, I do not find it totally convincing. To teach it as doctrine stretches Scripture somewhat in my opinion. To teach it as a possibility is well within reason, however. It could be that persons not mentioned in the Infallible Record lived past 1,000. But we do know that after the Fall the genetic barrier was enhanced. Mankind would die sooner. Well, except for Enoch and Elijah.

Another interesting discussion is the length of the year during the antediluvian (pre-flood) period. Bill Cooper of the CSM (Creation Science Movement) in the UK has written definitively on this. My recommendation is to get his books and see what you think. I could not begin to approach his level of scholarship on this subject. But the hypothesis is, if my memory serves me correctly, that pre-flood years were 360 days, and of course post flood they are around 365.25 days. As an aside, he has also broken down the Sumerian language of the Sumerian King list, and has come to some pretty dramatic conclusions concerning it, and the correlation of the names and years with these pre-Flood patriarchs. Sometimes he makes leaps of logic in my opinion from the evidence. But he is unparalleled in many areas, and for that I am thankful for his work. Also, on another note, Jared would have lived another 435 years after his son's ascension. Jared may have been an incredible parent. He certainly raised a dedicated child. Maybe he dedicated him to the Lord.

Genesis 5:21 "And Enoch lived sixty and five years, and begat Methuselah:"

Here we are! The translated man gives birth to the longest living individual in Scripture on this planet. Methuselah has entered the lexicon for extreme old age or length of years. God's countdown time clock has begun in this portion of Scripture. Methuselah means variously "When he dies, it shall come" speaking of the Flood, or alternately "son of the dart" by some. Maybe this records the arrow of God's judgment.

Methuselah would have been a contemporary with Adam for 243 years, and contemporaneous with Noah for 600 years. He was an incredible bridge from the Garden to the Flood. But we again are not sure if these Patriarch's ever spoke. Methuselah would have been born in approx. 3317 BC. Enoch, at 65, would have been relatively young for birthing a child at this period of time.

Genesis 5:22 "And Enoch walked with God after he begat Methuselah three hundred years, and begat sons and daughters:"

Much has been made of the phrase "walked with God after he begat Methuselah." Enoch lived 65 years, as the phrase goes with this section of genealogies. But then uniquely Enoch walks with God. And it says an event happened that caused the description to change. Methuselah was born. Was the sight of Enoch beholding the image of God, his own image, dramatic enough to change his life for God? Or, if this is the "Godly" Sethite line, did his dedication to God just stand out? Notice as well, he was able to walk with God while continuing to obey God and be fruitful and multiply. He need not become a monk or isolated. In 3769, Genesis 4:26, it says men began to call upon the name of the LORD. Now 452 years later it appears the revival has spread to Enoch. This verse could also mean (5:22) that Enoch continued walking with God after Methuselah's birth. So, some would say Enoch continued walking with God 300 years, indicating he walked with God for the times prior to Methuselah's birth. Others would look at Methuselah's birth as causative for Enoch walking with God.

Notice as well that Enoch did not just have a 1-time experience with God. He walked with Him. This is reminiscent of the Voice of the LORD walking in the Garden in Genesis 3:8. Walking is not sprinting. In Hebrews 12 we are to run with patience. Walking is a firm resolve to our destination. It is step by step. Later Abram would walk, trusting where he was going with faith in God. It is important to be saved by faith, but also important to walk by faith. It was a

300- year walk. 1 day with Jesus just is not enough to the soul in love with Him. Enoch was committed and dedicated, in this walk. Maybe Enoch's walk and prayers were enough to positively impact a great-grandson named Noah.

Genesis 5:23 "And all the days of Enoch were three hundred sixty and five years:"

One could make much that 365 years equals the number of days contained in a year. So, a week in Gen. 29:27, 28 and Daniel 9:27 would be a week of years. The time of Jacob's Trouble as mentioned in Jeremiah 30:7 also could be a week of years. So, the tribulation will be a week of years, or 7 years, and Enoch's catching away provides the key. Or maybe not. But we do know that something unique is about to happen to Enoch, that will not occur again for 2,000 plus years, until the time of Elijah. A man was about to cheat death (Hebrews 9:27). Enoch is seen as type of the rapture of the Church. God is coming back for a Church that is without spot, wrinkle or blemish, or any such thing. A dedicated Church. A holy Church. Like Enoch.

Others say Enoch will be one of the 2 witnesses in Revelation 11, along with Elijah. Sinful man must die. He never died, so he must come back and die. Is this an absolute rule? It is appointed unto men once to die. But many die more than once. Lazarus did. The widow of Nain's son did. The soldier that touched Elisha's bones did. Raptured saints will not, regardless of when you think the rapture is. So, I do not see that as an absolute rule that necessitates Enoch coming back to Earth to die.

Genesis 5:24 "And Enoch walked with God: and he was not; for God took him."

Enoch is mentioned thrice in the NT, in Luke, Hebrews, and Jude. Let us look at these NT references. The first, in Luke, is just mentioning Enoch is in the line of the Messiah, Jesus. In Hebrews he is mentioned in the great Hall of Fame of Faith. In Hebrews 11:5 we find, "By faith Enoch was translated that he should not see death; and was not found, because God had translated him: for before his translation he had this testimony, that he pleased God."

He is chronologically mentioned here, after Abel, and before Noah and Abraham. He is also connected with Hebrews 11:6, which reads, "But without faith it is impossible to please him: for he that cometh to God must believe that he is, and that he is a rewarder of them that diligently seek him." Notice that the end of verse 5 says that Enoch pleased God. Then at the beginning of verse 6 we see the word "please." And it mentions faith. This is clearly connecting verse 5 with verse 6. So, Enoch first of all believed God was. But he did not stop there. He also believed that God was a rewarder of them that diligently seek him. So, walking with God required faith to know God existed, and diligence to seek and walk with him. The next passage is fascinating and oft quoted.

In Jude 14 and 15 we see, "And Enoch also, the seventh from Adam, prophesied of these, saying, Behold, the Lord cometh with ten thousands of his saints," "To execute judgment upon all, and to convince all that are ungodly among them of all their ungodly deeds which they have ungodly committed, and of all their hard speeches which ungodly sinners have spoken against him." This is generally thought to be from 1 Enoch 1:9, though it is similar to Deuteronomy 33:2. Before we get into what Jude says about Enoch in history, let's get into the Book of Enoch.

The Book of Enoch is in 3 parts. The first is thought to be from the 3rd Century BC. The second from the 1st Century AD, and the third from the 5th AD, and it is clearly Jewish in nature. He is also mentioned in the Book of the Giants and the Wisdom of Sirach (44:16, Apocrypha) from around the 200's BC. Since Jude quotes Enoch authoritatively, many think the entire First Book of Enoch, or even all three of them, are inspired, and should be in the Canon. Since the first book is written in a Semitic language, and is endorsed by Jesus' half- brother, why isn't it inspired? First of all, NT authors quote at least 3 pagan authors in the New Testament (Acts 17:28; 1 Corinthians 15:33; and Titus 1:12. Some speculate others as well). This does not mean they are inspired, just that they were true in that particular case. Secondly, we are not even sure that Jude is quoting this book. He could have quoted a

Jewish Midrash of Deuteronomy 33:2, or an accurate oral tradition known at the time, or just receiving the words directly from God under the inspiration of the Holy Ghost. So, quotation, even if it is from Enoch, is not necessarily qualification for Canonical status. I have read a lot of Enoch, since this question was coming up so frequently. I see nothing which indicates canonicity or truthfulness. The Jews did have quite a legend built up about Enoch, however. They equated him with the angel Metatron, the angel that delivered the word of God. They also had him exalted above the Archangels, and in the direct presence of the Throne of God. All of this is pure speculation, of course. Sirach even seems to indicate Enoch was taken to the Garden of Eden.

Enoch was the seventh of the 10 generations mentioned in Genesis 5. He prophesied according to Jude. So, Enoch was a Prophet, evidently. He prophesied against evil people. Against false prophets. The LORD is coming with ten thousands of his saints. And He is going to execute judgment when He comes. This certainly looks like Revelation 19. And four times Enoch mentions the ungodly. In 2 Peter 2:5 it is mentioned that the Flood was brought upon the ungodly.

"And he was not" clearly means he was not here on Earth. Of course, he was in Heaven with God. Enoch was on this earth about five centuries less than the Patriarchs surrounding him, but what an impact he continues to have! May our lives have eternal impact upon others. Also, the phrase of the curse, "and he died" is missing from this great man's life. A man who walks with God does not lead a wasted life. Romans 5:14 seems fitting to quote here. It reads, "Nevertheless death reigned from Adam to Moses, even over them that had not sinned after the similitude of Adam's transgression, who is the figure of him that was to come." Does this mean Enoch never sinned? No, because the Scripture is emphatic that all have sinned and come short of the glory of God.

How did God take Enoch? We are not told, just as we are not told where God took him, and whether he would come back. Those events are considered less important to our knowledge than the fact that there is great reward in being faithful with God and walking with him. A whirlwind and a fiery chariot like Elijah perhaps? The Scripture is silent.

Genesis 5:25 "And Methuselah lived an hundred eighty and seven years, and begat Lamech:"

Enoch lived the shortest before having a child in this genealogy. Methuselah lived the longest to this point before begetting a child. He begets Lamech, which means "powerful." He is not to be confused with the Lamech from Cain's line in Chapter 4. There seems to have been an overlap of names, just as we have today. Lamech would have been born about 3130 BC, or 874 Anno Mundi (AM) – after the creation of the world. Lamech would have been contemporary with Adam for 56 years, and Seth 168 years. Again, we have no way of knowing if they ever communicated. By this time, several million people would have been around the world, probably. It is possible that Adam's Sethite progeny would have been centered together, but we do not know that. We are not even sure exactly what the antediluvian world looked like on a continental scale. Lamech would have been able to live 113 years contemporary with his Godly grandfather Enoch.

Genesis 5:26 "And Methuselah lived after he begat Lamech seven hundred eighty and two years, and begat sons and daughters:"

Gematria, as mentioned previously, is a Jewish reckoning of numbers, and their meaning. Looking at these numbers through gematria may be fascinating, and hold certain truths, but I have done very little in this realm of study. You may feel led to do so. When visiting Israel, on the Sea of Galilee, our Jewish Christian boat operator said 153, the number of fish that the apostles caught in John 21, represented Elohim to the Jews. So possibly the ages that are mentioned here have some significance as well. The Bible is so vast, it can never be fully plumbed in one lifetime, yet simple enough that a child can understand its eternal truths. So, Methuselah, quite like Abraham later, after God healed his body, it appears had children for the remainder of his life. Could you imagine what it would be like to have an older sibling four centuries your elder? Or a younger sibling, multiple centuries younger than you? Also, the amount of wisdom and knowledge must have been prolific for people near millennia old. But satan would also have centuries to observe people to understand overall tendencies in the human race. And oh, how he has used them against us, his wicked, vile, evil devices. Evil and vile are the same letters, just arranged differently, by the way.

Genesis 5:27 "And all the days of Methuselah were nine hundred sixty and nine years: and he died."

Unlike his father Enoch, the dreaded words "he died" are appended to the saga of Methuselah's life. Possibly he trained Lamech well in the art of child rearing, for Lamech's child would be a great example of living for God, as his great-grandfather Enoch was.

Now Methuselah would have died in 2348 BC, the year of the Flood. He would have outlived his son Lamech by 5 years. Notice that Methuselah died. It does not say destroyed in the Flood. So, he evidently died a natural death, and when he died, it, the Flood came.

Genesis 5:28 "And Lamech lived an hundred eighty and two years, and begat a son:"

Both Methuselah and Lamech were late starters, evidently, in beginning a family. This will continue with Noah. Noah was born about 2948 BC., 14 years after the death of Seth, and 69 years after the ascension of Enoch. Noah means "rest." In this genealogical section, all the first mentioned are sons. I am assuming due to Messianic genealogy, that all of these were firstborns, as previously mentioned. I have not thought through if that is an absolute necessity, again as I have previously mentioned. This is only the second time in this chapter, and all of Scripture, the phrase "begat a son" is used.

Genesis 5:29 "And he called his name Noah, saying, This same shall comfort us concerning our work and toil of our hands, because of the ground which the LORD hath cursed."

Being 182, Lamech was already feeling the effects of fighting against the Fall in order to eat. Leftover produce would have been sold or traded to those who did not till the cursed soil. This would seem to be the birth of capitalism. Excess capital is used to purchase goods and services. It seems to be the most natural way God intended things to work. The goods could have been produced by wicked people, possibly in the lineage of Cain, but this capitalistic strain would still work. 2 Thessalonians 3:10 seems to continue with this principle when it says, "For even when we were with you, this we commanded you, that if any would not work, neither should he eat."

The use of the word "us" is intriguing. If Noah was his firstborn, it may indicate Lamech and his wife. But it would be plausible that it is speaking to more than just those 2. This does give credence to the possibility that this line of Patriarchs mentioned in Chapter 5 did live in close proximity to one another. And with Enoch being translated, a worker would be missing. But that would likely have negligible impact on the numbers of people that Chapter 5 implicates would have been alive. But another worker, Noah, would necessarily be valuable, especially as arable land became scarcer with the exponential growth of the population. In Chapter 6, we will observe, LORD willing, some of the events vexing the Earth at this time, that would lead to the Flood of Judgement.

Some see in Noah's name, "comfort" or "rest," as a symbol or type of the Holy Ghost. There are certainly grounds for validity in this. But I am not sure how far along that type would play out. On another note, Lamech was privileged to have 23 words of Holy Writ recorded that he spoke. That is .0029% of all the 788,258 words in the Bible. And one of those words is LORD. Now, that also may give us a clue on whether this Sethite line was primarily Godly. Lamech believed the Scripture. He knew the ground was cursed by Jehovah. He had not veered into false doctrine.

This is the first use of the name Noah (or Noe as it is 5 times in the NT, being the Greek spelling). It is found in 51 verses, being used 58 times. During the Exodus, we find it is also the name of a woman, the daughter of Zelophehad.

Genesis 5:30 "And Lamech lived after he begat Noah five hundred ninety and five years, and begat sons and daughters:"

"Begat sons and daughters" is a phrase found 9 times in this chapter and is not found again until Chapter 11 (vs. 11), where it is found eight times in that chapter. Lamech begat sons and daughters, but none were as famous as Noah. Also, unless they died prematurely, or were taken like Enoch, they all died in the Flood except for Noah. This is a classic example of the firstborn being able to stand against the wiles of an evil society, and even against his entire family to serve God. Noah, his wife, and his sons and their wives made it onto the ark. But the rest of his siblings did not make it. They were punished in the worldwide Deluge. Fascinatingly, in Ken Johnson's edition of the book of Jasher, in which he makes a very good case for at least its semi-accuracy, it is recorded that birth control and abortion were rampant before the Flood. Interesting reading, but I put no stock in it. If God would have wanted us to know that on a certain scale, it would be in Holy Writ.

Genesis 5:31 "And all the days of Lamech were seven hundred seventy and seven years: and he died."

If all numbers mean something in Scripture, then 777 should certainly merit our attention. Did he do a perfect job raising Noah? Was he overtly righteous? We really see no indication of that in the 23 words he spoke in verse 29. Converted to holiness like Enoch, possibly with the birth of his son? Not sure. I am not even certain that was the causative factor of Enoch's holiness walk. All we can really be certain about this is the repetitive nature of the phrase, "and he died." Possibly, if seven is the number of completeness as some assert, that his death symbolized the completing of God's mercy on the Antediluvian world. Another possibility is the fact that Lamech could have had a positive impact of Noah's children.

Genesis 5:32 "And Noah was five hundred years old: and Noah begat Shem, Ham, and Japheth."

I have heard it taught that Noah's sons were triplets. That seems not to be the case. We do know in Genesis 10:21 Japheth is called the elder. In Genesis 11:10 Shem was 100 when Arphaxad was born 2 years after the Flood. So, in this verse, the birth order is seemingly not followed when listing Noah's sons. Whether this has implications for other parts of the genealogy, I am not certain. But it does seem to be irrefutable here. It would also strongly indicate that Ham was the youngest son, unless Mrs. Noah had 3 sons in 3 consecutive years, which is possible. But most probably the birth order is Japheth, Shem, and Ham.

Shem is where the term "Semitic" comes from. We use it still, which is a great testament to Scriptures' accuracy. Josephus records that Shem's sons founded Elam, Lydia, Levantine, Assyria, and Chaldea. Many Jews assert that Shem was Melchizedek. In early Islam, he was considered to be a part of Muhammed's lineage. Shem means "heard by God." Deuteronomy 6:4 is called the Shema, or the "hear."

Japheth means most probably "to expand" or "beautiful." He is considered to be the founder of Europe, basically. Genealogies are found in Genesis Chapter 10, and the places Noah's progeny founded. Many sources seem to relate that "Jupiter" comes from a corruption of his name.

Ham may mean either "servant" or "royalty." There is no indication that his name means "black" as the false Hamitic Curse theory would hypothesize. His descendants would have founded Africa and parts of the Ancient Near East.

Mrs. Noah. Again, the study of pivotal persons in Scripture whose names are not mentioned is a fascinating study. Some Jewish literature says she was Naamah. Ancient Anglo-Saxon literature calls her "Percoba." Other names are Emzara (Book of Jubilees), Haikal, Barthenos, Nemzar, Amzurah, Set, Dalila, Phiapharra, Tytea, and Norea (Nag Hammadi Gnostic literature). Tobit 4:12 says it was one of Noah's own kindred. Jubilee's mentions it was Methuselah's granddaughter. I would say she is anonymous.

The three wives of Shem, Ham, and Japheth likewise have a legendary history. The famous Sibylline Oracles claim to be written by Noah's daughter in law Sambethe. Evidently the 3 daughters-in-law according to this lived incredibly long lives, and Sambethe moved to Greece 900 years after the Flood and began writing. Her father is identified as Gnostos (how interesting) and her mother as Circe. Isis and Sabba were her sisters. Other names from various sources are Pandora, Noela, and Noegla, Parsia, Cataphua, and Fura, Salib, Nahlib, and Arbasisah. Shem's wife is also known as Leah. Bill Cooper and John Gill are great sources of information for this, as well as Wikipedia.

We also notice it does not mention Noah having other sons or daughters at this point. Neither does it mention his sons having pre-flood children. It is literally Noah and his family versus the world.

Genesis 6

THIS IS ONE OF THE MOST FASCINATING chapters in Scripture. We are not sure exactly what time period it covers, only that it ends around 2448 BC. It began when men began to multiply upon the earth (verse 1). In this chapter are tales of giants, sons of God, violence, illicit liaisons, grace, and Divine visitation. To say that this is the prelude to a pivotal point in Earth's history would be a supreme understatement.

Verse 1 "And it came to pass, when men began to multiply on the face of the earth, and daughters were born unto them,"

A population explosion is seen here. With the comma at the end of the verse, it is natural to take verses 1 and 2 together.

Verse 2 "That the sons of God saw the daughters of men that they were fair; and they took them wives of all which they chose."

The B'nai Elohim, the sons of God. One of the most controversial Scriptures in the Bible. Traditional Jewish interpretation is that these are angels, who saw the beauty of the Pre-Flood women, and took wives of all which they chose. This also may indicate polygamy. Were the Sons of God so powerful, that the men of the time were unable to stop them? Were these the famous Anunnaki of Sumerian lore, who taught men about weapons of war, and women to paint their face? Zecharia Sitchin has much on them, and M. D. Treece, the eminent Biblical linguist from Lake Charles studied them intently as well, even learning Sumerian.

The most natural reading would be that the sons of God were the line of Seth that were Godly. Chapter 4 has Cain's lineage, Chapter 5 Seth's. We have seen some evidence that Seth's lineage was Godly, culminating with Noah, but including Enoch, and possibly others. This has been the traditional conservative Christian view over the years.

Another view is that Adam and Eve had children in the Garden before the Fall. And these unfallen children were referred to as the sons of God. We have seen the evidence for pre-Fall childbirth in Genesis 3.

Among Bible believers, these are really the 3 dominant theories, with the first 2 being the most popular. The biggest problems I have with the angel theory are:

1) Is this a second fall of the angels? Did 1/3 fall with Lucifer, and another batch later? Or are these part of the 1/3 who fell with Lucifer? There seems to be a split among some concerning this. Were demons called sons of God? That is why some think there was a second fall of angels, because of the intractableness of this view. Some would say due to the law of First Reference that this has to be angels, since angels are referred to as B'nai Elohim in Job 38:6. But during the course of this study, we have periodically pointed out the weakness of this supposed law of Biblical interpretation. It just does not hold up consistently.

2) Can spirit beings' mate with humans? Do they think in human categories, like women being fair? We know from Hebrews 1 that angels are spirits. Though they may be able to eat (in manna, man did eat angel's food), does this mean they also have reproductive capabilities? Matthew 22:30 says, "For in the resurrection they neither marry, nor are given in marriage, but are as the angels of God in heaven." The retort is that they are not in heaven, but on earth, and have procreative abilities. But how would falling from Heaven

make them have reproductive capacities? And they did not just have sexual liaisons with women, they took them as wives. So, this is a big problem. Some try to reference this occurring during Greek mythology for justification that this was indeed possible. But I would not want to base theology on pagan mythology. Now of course they would segue in passages of Scripture from Jude and 2 Peter as well. While you could interpret those Scriptures in favor of angels, I do not see it as a necessity as some do. It could just as easily in context be speaking of other things.

Now some say that these were demon possessed men, or temporarily demon possessed men, who married these women. And the demons corrupted the human DNA. Interesting, but how?

The sons of Seth theory has problems as well. Why would their godly DNA cause giants to be born? And how did giants get in Canaan several centuries after the Flood? The general explanation is that Ham's wife was impregnated by the sons of God and carried this offspring through the flood. But there is no evidence for this, other than it is Ham's seed that is usually associated with giants later in the Pentateuch.

There are so many problems with the first 2 theories, I am almost left with theory 3 as being closest to the truth by default. These pre-Fall humans, being born before the corruption of DNA at the Fall, would have been huge like Adam was (probably). Possibly Adam and Eve only had man children before the Fall. And this race of Sons of God saw post-Fall women, had children, who were also large. And once they died, their offspring would have been considered huge, and legends would have grown up around them. But I love and have fellowship with people of all 3 views. This is one of those discussion points in Scripture. Romans 14 says we can sincerely disagree on some things.

One other point is that some would say "wives" is here mistranslated. I would say this is just an attempt to fit an interpretation into Scripture rather than vice versa.

Genesis 6:3 "And the LORD said, My spirit shall not always strive with man, for that he also is flesh: yet his days shall be an hundred and twenty years."

This passage has multiple interpretations as well. Some say this is setting a 120-year limit on man's lifespan. Others say that God has limits in His mercy, and from the time this Scripture was appropriated until the Flood would be 120 years. Therefore people say that Noah was a preacher of righteousness for 120 years. God's Spirit is holy. So, it would not strive with man's sinfulness. Notice He said "man," not hybrid, not angel, etc. That is significant. And flesh, not spirit as angels are. We know that spirits have not flesh and blood.

But it could also mean the spirit in man that God created. And that this conscience in man would not strive with man sinning constantly. Whichever of the interpretations is correct, it is settled. Trouble is coming. God is significantly dealing with humans. "And Jehovah said" is how this passage begins.

Genesis 6:4 "There were giants in the earth in those days; and also after that, when the sons of God came in unto the daughters of men, and they bare children to them, the same became mighty men which were of old, men of renown."

This is another verse that lends credence to the possibility of the sons of God being offspring of Adam and Eve before the Fall. There were giants. Then after that, there were more giants after that the sons of God came in unto the daughters of men and had children. They became mighty men, men of old, men of renown. This seems to be the stuff of legends. But consider, there were giants before the sons of God came into the daughters of men. Un-fallen children of Adam and Eve? Quite possibly.

Another lesson we do not need to lose in this: The sons of God looked on the daughters of men that they were fair. As it was in the days of Noe, so shall it be in the days of the coming of the Son of Man. The sons of God, the Church, needs to be careful not to look on the beauty of the lost women in the world. Pornography and sins of the eyes are prevalent today. A point to consider. Hat tip to Franklin Smith for that observation.

Genesis 6:5 "And GOD saw that the wickedness of man was great in the earth, and that every imagination of the thoughts of his heart was only evil continually."

"For as he thinketh in his heart, so is he: ...," so says Solomon in Proverbs 23:7. This is also the basis of one of the most popular Christian self-help books ever written, by James Allen. This is true of every person. N. A. Urshan used to say our thoughts speak as loud in heaven as our words. Man was wicked because his imagination of the thoughts of his heart was wicked. Jeremiah tells us, "The heart is deceitful above all things, and desperately wicked: who can know it?" Jeremiah 17:9. Solomon once again states, "He that trusteth in his own heart is a fool:" Proverbs 28:26. Matthew and Mark record a total of 14 things that come out of a man's heart. Jesus said this is what defiles a man. So the sons of God saw in verse 2. Now God sees. Mankind was wicked. It was everywhere. Every person except for Noah and his small tribe contributed to this. Noah's brothers and sisters evidently did. Man, through conscience, and Noah's preaching knew the difference between right and wrong. God's Spirit strove with them. Possibly there were other preachers during this time. Lamech, Methuselah, Enoch. A written Word? You could see the Garden of Eden. You could look at the Cherubim and the flaming sword guarding the entrance. Yet man sinned. He rebelled. Satan had seemingly won. But a seed would be saved, and that seed would eventually give birth to Messiah some 54 generations hence according to some calculations of the genealogical reckoning. The Lukan account and the Genesis genealogies are a discussion for another time, God willing.

Man had overspread the earth. His wickedness was not confined to Mesopotamia. This was not a localized flood. Billions lived at this time. The Earth was overspread with people. And with sin. So, the Flood had to be universal. It was a type of baptism. It washed away the wicked so the "Rest" or "Comfort" would remain.

Let us look at the second part of this verse. Sometimes it is quoted quickly but not considered. Every imagination. This is visualization. This is the inward territory of idolatry and strongholds. These imaginations were thoughts. They were not classical thinking. They were not considerations. This was not learned discussion. This was not reading and pondering. This was images. Lust, violence, lies. Man was out of control. The New Birth was not given yet to control him. He was a savage beast, red in tooth and claw, just the way satan wanted the image of God to be. And mankind thought these evil thoughts, entertained these evil images continually. There was no stopping point. Mankind was wholly given to evil at this point. We can see hints of this in the world today, becoming like a raging fire. As Kipling remarked of civilization, how dark the night, how thin the veneer. A blood lust like the Soviet Union, Pol Pot, Mao, Hitler's henchmen, the French Revolution, Ustashi death squads, Hutu and Tutsi so easily sweeps mankind. In an instant. And it is fatal. "As it was in the days of Noe," Jesus said.

Man went to bed lustful, covetous, violent, rapacious, and he awakened that way. Mankind with no restraints is a vicious creature. Talk to those who have been on the frontlines of war, and its aftermath. No doubt the long lifespans of mankind contributed to them being able to devolve into a worse and worse state.

Genesis 6:6 "And it repented the LORD that he had made man on the earth, and it grieved him at his heart."

God repents. Moses told God to repent one time. There are other times God repented. Of course, you must nuance that. God is the LORD, He changes not. He obviously does not repent the way man does. God, in His foreknowledge, knew man would get to this point. But seeing it play out in time, it hurt God, who is love, so bad in His heart, He wished He had never made man, in a certain sense. But of course, in another sense, it is the unfolding drama of redemption where He saves a bride for Himself to be with Him throughout all eternity.

Notice "made" and "create" are synonymous in these first few chapters of Genesis by and large. Notice God as well has emotions.

Since we are in the image of God, this is where we get our emotions from. Temperance is the right management of emotions. God loved us so much, He hated us to be enslaved to sin. The punishment of sin is death. So worldwide sin would result in a worldwide flood of punishment. Water is a miracle. It has 74 unique properties and is necessary for life. It is a cleansing agent. And what is necessary for life will be used for death here.

Now did God have a heart? In the Spiritual emotive sense, yes. But He did not have a flesh and blood heart until the Man Jesus Christ.

God knew. Openeness Theology, which says God is not omniscient, but rather subject to the whims of man's free choice, is to be rejected. He was just frustrated. Holiness and love were in Divine tension. Luke 15 has beautiful illustrations of this. Job 22:15-18 seems to recount this time-period. In it we read:

Verse 15 "Hast thou marked the old way which wicked men have trodden?"

Verse 16 "Which were cut down out of time, whose foundation was overflown with a flood:"

Verse 17 "Which said unto God, Depart from us: and what can the Almighty do for them?"

Verse 18 "Yet he filled their houses with good things: but the counsel of the wicked is far from me."

Genesis 6:7 "And the LORD said, I will destroy man whom I have created from the face of the earth; both man, and beast, and the creeping thing, and the fowls of the air; for it repenteth me that I have made them."

Who was Jehovah speaking to? Himself? The angels? Future generations? Scripture? Notice the "I." Jehovah is a Singular "I', and He created man (Genesis 1:26, 27). But it is not just man, but beast, creeping thing, and fowls of the air that will be destroyed. And once again God says it repenteth Him. In verse 6 it grieved Him at His heart, as well.

Repentance has a connotation of sorrow, as well as change of direction. Old timers wanted to see tears at repentance.

God here speaks 37 words specifically. And it is the death sentence of mankind, and all life upon earth. The fossils will be formed. Many of the fossils are petrified in the state of struggle, or violent death. Their backs arched, showing instantaneous burial, fish in the act of eating other fish. Mammoths with undigested daisies in their bellies, frozen solid in the cataclysm. Animals of all classes fossilized together on high ground. All indicate rapid burial.

How must it have grieved God's Heart to destroy His own image. To reach the point to make that decision. Of course, in His Omniscience, He knew it would come to that. But God still feels. He has emotions. As we shall see in verse 10, man was bent on destroying himself. God destroyed the many before they destroyed all. Did God supernaturally preserve Noah and his family from the angry denizens of earth? Or where they simply ignored in the pleasure fest of flesh? And let me point out once again at the beginning of this verse that God "created" man, and at the end of the verse, He had "made" them. Create and made are so often synonyms. I only bring this out because proponents of the Gap theory make much of the differences between the two words. And on rare occasions, there are differences. But that is the exception, not the rule. And certainly not overwhelmingly enough to build a doctrine on.

Genesis 6:8 "But Noah found grace in the eyes of the LORD."

"Rest," as Noah's name means found grace. This does not mean that Noah was evil, with wicked imaginations and full of violence and God just sovereignly chose him to be saved. That is not the implication at all. Noah was serving God. And as such, Jehovah's eyes found him, and His eyes were full of grace. Verse 9 will expound on this.

A couple of verses on the eyes of God, and on the grace of God may help with interpretation and setting.

2 Chronicles 16:9a "For the eyes of the LORD run to and fro throughout the whole earth, to shew himself strong in the behalf of them whose heart is perfect toward him…"

Titus 2:11, 12 "For the grace of God that bringeth salvation hath appeared to all men,"

"Teaching us that, denying ungodliness and worldly lusts, we should live soberly, righteously, and godly, in this present world;"

The eye is incredibly complex. Paul Brand, in the Christian Classic "In His Image" goes into indefatigable detail of the complexities of the eye, and the impossibilities for it to have evolved. Darwin recognized this, and the situation is no better today for the evolutionist. Though theories of Tribolyte, Mollusk, and Octopus eyes are relied upon to prop up an evolutionary development of the eye, at the end of the day, it is an impossibility. And the objective deep thinker knows this. God is omniscient. He sees everything at once. Nothing is hid from the eyes of Him with whom we have to do. As brilliant and complex as our eyes are, they pale to Him that is the Omniscient One.

Genesis 6:9 "These are the generations of Noah: Noah was a just man and perfect in his generations, and Noah walked with God."

This is the second usage of the phrase "these are the generations." Some speculate that these are clay tablets that Moses consulted. I see no reason for that conclusion. At 10:1 we will see the generations of Noah's sons. In 11:10, Shem is specifically mentioned with this phraseology. And in 11:27, it is Terah, focusing in on a certain family. A Messianic line.

Noah was just. This is something God lauds. He sits upon the throne of justice (Ps. 89:14). Proverbs speaks oft of the just (it is dealt with at least 21 times in Proverbs). He was even handed in his dealings with others and himself. And he did not violate God's laws of justice. Of course, he sinned, all have. But he was doing what he could. The old timers would speak oft of direction. Are you trying, or are you heading off the straight and narrow? There is a difference between veering off course, and falling down on your way to Heaven, as Christian showed us in Pilgrims Progress. "For a just man falleth seven times, and riseth up again: but the wicked shall fall into mischief." says Proverbs 24:16. "Rejoice not against me, O mine enemy: when I fall, I shall arise;" Micah 7:8a.

Noah was perfect in his generations. Many take this to mean he did not have seed corrupted with the sons of God and the daughters of men. Others say that none of the Cainite lineage was found in his bloodline. Others would say that he walked with God in his dealings with his extended family, going backwards to Enos, Cainan, Mahalaleel, Jared and the like. One, two, or all of these may be true. But since he was in the line of Messiah, it was necessary for his lineage to not be corrupted. Of course, everyone currently alive, or that has lived in the past 4 plus millennia have Noah's DNA.

But we come to another important fact, found in his great-grandfather Enoch, whom Noah never met at the time; Noah walked with God. Every day Noah had a relationship with God. I am not sure why it is so difficult for Christians to walk with God. We have more than they did, the Spirit dwelling within in the New Birth. A Bible to hold in its entirety. Something that seems so simple, so obvious, so blessed, is such a struggle. Satan continues to switch the price tags.

The Voice of the LORD walked in the Garden in the cool of the day. Jews prayed at 3 p.m. in NT times. God calls us away to be with Him. It is a blessing, not legalism.

Notice Noah walked with God when the world did not. Daniel walked with God even when they passed a law against it. David walked with God. Do not let the world conform you into its mold, but be transformed, and transform this world. The world does not need any more sinners, it has plenty. It needs more saints. Those that will walk with God.

Genesis 6:10 "And Noah begat three sons, Shem, Ham, and Japheth."

We are re-introduced to Shem, Ham, and Japheth. Shem, though not the oldest, is first, possibly because it is, he in the Messianic line. These 3 sons would presumably help Noah with the building project and be beneficial in a more rapid increase of population in the Post-Diluvian world. In 9:1 God told Noah, along with his sons, to be fruitful and multiply, and replenish the earth, yet it is not recorded that Noah had more children. Mrs. Noah could have been barren after giving birth to these 3, or Noah could have been impotent. The atmospheric change may have been so drastic that the elderly could no longer have children as before the Flood. Or Noah could have found means to disobey God, though this seems unlikely due to Noah walking with God, unless he backslid through the Flood somehow. But Scripture is silent. We should be likewise in dogmatic terms.

Genesis 6:11 "The earth also was corrupt before God, and the earth was filled with violence."

The term "corrupt" used here means to decay or mar. Many think this refers to the sons of God mingling corrupt seed. I think it merely means that mankind had violated God's laws. They were living opposite of God's holiness. And once again we see the theme of violence. I do find it interesting that in English we see the root "viol" in violence. The word "viol" is associated with Lucifer in Ezekiel 28 and is a musical instrument, but I have not been able to find an etymological connection in English or Hebrew. But it does not mean it is not there. It does mean I have not found it. But I have not searched exhaustively, either. Maybe you can find definitive evidence either way. Violence was not just part of the earth's existence; the earth was filled with it. I am assuming this means person on person and did not necessarily apply to the animal kingdom. I would also think that this does not apply exclusively to war, either. Violence, the turning of the image of God upon one another, was rampant. Whether for rapine, sport, war, covetousness, it was consuming the earth. The weapons of the Anunnaki, or fallen angels, were doing their work, if that is indeed where they came from. God is the Author of Peace, the Prince of Peace. Romans 1 and Jude are good places to look at the natural order, the God given order, being corrupted.

Genesis 6:12 "And God looked upon the earth, and, behold, it was corrupt; for all flesh had corrupted his way upon the earth."

Verse 13 will once again make a connection between the corruption and violence. Original intent had been violated. Again, some associate this with genetic contamination. But this could also emphasize the natural order was violated. Elohim looks down upon earth. All flesh had corrupted his way. Flesh is referred to here as "his." It was free choice. The carnal had conquered. The final end of man is to destroy himself. Nietzsche spoke of "the will to power" once God is dead in the minds of man. Man had no purpose other than to conquer fellow man. There was no empathy. Evil communications corrupt good manners. The line of Cain had won. It had corrupted the Godly line. Evil actions spread like a contagion, since they lie inherent in our sinful natures waiting to be awakened. When something is corrupt, so often it smells. The earth stunk with violation of man injuring God's image in man. God does not necessarily have to destroy man. Given a long enough time, it seems man destroys himself. Sin must be resisted. The cultural Marxists said that American Culture would stink. It is in the process today. We need a deep repentance after deeply revolting from our God. The totality and finality of this corruption before God is shocking. From Eden to destruction in nine generations. The longevity of man had allowed him to descend all the more rapidly. He would live long enough to be terribly corrupt through centuries of living.

Genesis 6:13 "And God said unto Noah, 'The end of all flesh is come before me; for the earth is filled with violence through them; and, behold, I will destroy them with the earth.'"

God speaks to Noah here through verse 21. This is the longest discourse God has with anyone in the first few chapters of Genesis. Notice God places all the blame on mankind. Not the annunaki, not demons, not satan, not predestination, but all of mankind except Noah and his family, presumably. They want to do violence with each other, so God helps them and speeds up the process, in judgment. He brings the violence to its ultimate end, death. Hardening a heart is a similar process. If someone wants to harden their heart, God will resist for a while, then he assists them. If they will not have the love of the truth, God will send them a lie to believe.

Bloodlust and blood sports were clearly shunned in the early Church. Christians did not attend the games or go to the Colosseum, at least not voluntarily. How did Paul use such sports and military analogies, then? Well, they were ubiquitous throughout the Empire. Paul knew about them. Paul need not sanction or participate in them to use them as illustrations that would be common to all. And did he have a choice? It was inspired writing, after all.

Also, when God said that the end of all flesh is come before Him, it could mean that if He didn't intervene, mankind would kill themselves, not necessarily that He would be the One doing the killing, though I think that interpretation is tenuous at best. So, saving Noah and his family, in any case, was an act of mercy. The earth is filled with violence through the people of the world, including Noah's brothers and sisters quite possibly, but not Noah.

Genesis 6:14 "Make thee an ark of gopher wood; rooms shalt thou make in the ark, and shalt pitch it within and without with pitch."

First, we notice God pronounced judgment. Then He begins to make the provision for salvation. He does not make suggestions to Noah. God knows best. These are commands. And since Noah walked with God, it was assumed and known by God that Noah would obey these commands. Adam should have walked with God. Enoch did, and so did Noah. Three commands are given in this particular verse. First, make an ark of gopher wood. Not any type of wood will do. We see this repeated throughout Scripture that God makes specific commands. Arbitrary obedience is death. Not just any type of sacrifice will do in the Law. It must be according to order. It must be on a particular day. It must be a particular amount, a particular type of animal, a particular way, and the like. There is one door to the tabernacle. One door into the ark. This salvation for Noah must be of gopher wood. And it is for Noah's own good. His salvation. Possibly the Cross was of gopher wood?

Second, the ark was to have rooms. Four rooms for each of the four families on the ark, possibly. Rooms probably for each type of animal. Rooms for food, possibly waste disposal, and supplies. And next it must be pitched within and without with pitch. Bitumen, a type of asphalt, was to seal the ark. Some have noted that this would make the ark black in color within and without. We are reminded of Jesus, a type of this ark. He who knew no sin became sin for us. And the darkness within the ark would allow for a semi-hibernative state to be on the animals within. Others have observed that the word pitch, "kaphar," is used most often in Scripture as the word for atonement (71 times) or reconciliation.

We also observe the "thee/them" contrast of verses 13 and 14. Judgment for them, mercy for thee. Some will be lost, and others will be saved. We need also to focus on the fact that God never changed His plan of salvation based on numbers. It was a big ark, but only eight are saved. Only those within, not those around it. The door was open. Noah was preaching. It was for whosoever will. But God did not change His plan based on lack of participation. We are the ones to change, not God. As Jesus said of New Testament salvation many would seek to enter in and would not be able (Luke 13:24). In Moses' day, the way was open to the Promised Land for all who came out of Egypt with Moses. Only Caleb and Joshua made it. Hebrews 3:16-18 explains this process.

Reason, result, provision. God is explaining. The reason is man's sin. The result is God's judgment. The provision is God's mercy. God could have allowed Noah to levitate for the designated period of time or carried him to Heaven with Enoch, temporarily. But He chose this way. This was a worldwide flood, not a local disaster. Water seeks its own level. God did not send Noah 1,000 miles away to escape local judgment. He sent him into an ark because it was to be worldwide judgment. Local flood proponents really do not have a leg to stand upon, either in language or logic of the Text. The Earth was filled with violence, not just the Ancient Near East.

Formed wood with atonement on it definitely looks toward the Cross. But as a type, does this mean that the Cross was made of gopher wood? Not necessarily. Types are many times not that specific. But what was gopher wood then? Petrified gophers? Trees gophers lived around? This is its only use in Scripture. The Hebrew word interestingly enough is "gopher," so accounts for the pitch. The pitch was for sealing. There was to be no leaks in this boat. The fate of future mankind depended on it.

Genesis 6:15 "And this is the fashion which thou shalt make it of: The length of the ark shall be three hundred cubits, the breadth of it fifty cubits, and the height of it thirty cubits."

As I suspect that cubits were quite a bit larger before the Flood, the traditional 450x75x45 ft. dimensions for the ark is too small. The flora and fauna we find from ancient times is known as megafauna, because it is so large. Some of the reliefs we find from after the Flood are huge in their scale, such as rulers holding tigers and such. In the ancient world, there were three types of cubits, a traditional, a Babylonian, and an Egyptian. One was 18 inches, the others were 21 and 26.5 inches, measured from the hand to the elbow. But in the Antediluvian world of long lifespans and a more perfect world with less DNA mutative accretions, I would highly suspect that mankind was larger. Wasn't Adam 60 ft. tall in the Koran? I am not too sure that is all that fanciful. But even if we are talking of 10-15 ft. individuals, the cubit would have been much larger. Stonehenge as well as other ancient monuments seem to attest to larger individuals in ancient times. So, the computations of volume, that already show the ark was more than sufficient to save everything alive in the numbers mentioned in Scripture, would be even larger. Reptiles never quit growing. So, with them having lifespans 10 times plus longer than they do now, if it were similar to humans in the Pre-Flood times, they would be enormous. But younger, smaller reptiles could have been brought aboard the ark. Some may even have been classed as dinosaurs. Tarantulas, wasps, frogs, turtles, lice, scorpions aboard the ark? I assume they were all there as well. Maybe their temperament was different in the Pre-Flood world.

Scientists tell us this is the perfect size for a vessel. In simulations, these Biblical dimensions of the ark propel the ship into waves, making for a much more level experience. It would have been nearly impossible for the ark to capsize. Here we see to the fallacy of the fanciful tales of mythology, with Utnapishtim in a cube ark, that simulations say would have spun like a top, killing all aboard in short order. No, the Bible is correct down to the most minute details. And notice Scripture as well continually gives us these details. It is willing to be tested and verified. Truthful documents are willing to be verified. They have the ring of truth about them.

God placed a large responsibility upon Noah. While he was preaching, he was to be working. It reminds us of Paul as a tentmaker. God could have made the boat. But He entrusted Noah with the task. It had to be precise, just as the tabernacle was. When the tabernacle was complete, made perfect as God gave the design, the Glory of God filled it. God wants us to not deviate from His Word one iota.

Let's look at some issues others point out about the Flood. Most of these are very practical issues, but none are intractable. Such as, how did plants survive the Flood? Either they were onboard the ark, or some floated during the destruction, to later be planted, or a combination of both. How did fresh and saltwater fish survive the Flood? Saltwater and fresh would have sought out their different levels, as they have different densities. And many fish can live in brackish water or can adapt rapidly. But the ones that needed specialization would have just found their level with either the fresh or salt water in it. We also cannot overlook the supernatural care and provenance of God in preserving plants and animals. How did amphibians survive? I would assume they were on the ark, and maybe Noah had a special environment for them, with, dirt and water. How did air get to all three levels of the ark? Certainly, there were connections between floors, especially if Noah and his family had to do any type of maintenance. So, air could have circulated freely. Was saltwater the water of judgment? Many have adjudicated this to be so, but I am not sure of that. But it is an interesting discussion.

Fossils found in the middle of the ocean of land dwelling creatures, fossils found of fish eating other fish, animals of all types mangled together on high ground, and even mass fossilization itself all provide ample evidence for the Flood. Many fossils are found with their backs arched, in a sudden death by suffocation mode. The Grand Canyon, polystrate fossils, fossils in coal beds, oil fields, fossils on top of mountains and in the Sahara Desert all show the results of this great worldwide Deluge. Walt Brown, PhD from MIT, has shown many of the results of the Flood to the earth's crust. There is still much more water under the earth's crust than above. Dr. Brown would even explain comets and meteors based on the titanic changes that occurred on earth during the Flood, and the water's force exploding from deep underground pushing rocks upward with enough force to exit our atmosphere. His detailed, scientific analysis is worthy of exploration. His book is entitled "In the Beginning." It has gone through eight editions, and I have heard a 9th may coming soon.

Genesis 6:16 "A window shalt thou make to the ark, and in a cubit shalt thou finish it above; and the door of the ark shalt thou set in the side thereof; with lower, second, and third stories shalt thou make it."

More details are given about the ark. The window of course would have been a necessity. Would Noah have been able to look out and see the floating devastation, like the priests could see the blood in the water in the laver of the tabernacle? Probably not. Noah was unable to see the ground once the ark had landed. It appears God spared him the horror of looking at the judgment for man's sin. The Israelite Priesthood did see that horror, with the slain sacrificial animals. Noah, when finally exiting the ark, could just look upon the Earth, new, and with the curse removed. The window of the ark would have been for air and would have possibly gone the length of the ark, with the ability to open it in sections. Noah did have 100 years to build the ark, and I am sure the technological knowhow for the ark's construction was available. And again, let us not overlook the supernatural help of God available to Noah. And thank the Lord for boys, I am sure Noah must have thought! So, with the window a cubit above, it would not have allowed the waves to splash in the ark. Air would come in but not water. Ingenious. But actually it was just of God. And the window would have allowed the smells to go out while it brought in fresh air. It stunk on the ark, possibly. But it was much better in the ark than in the world. The same is true of the Church. It may stink in the Church sometimes, but it is infinitely better than the alternative.

The door to the ark was in its side. Eve came from Adam's side. Jesus' side was pierced at Calvary. The ark had three stories. Possibly the door was hinged. But again, this is an ingenious design. Animals on one level, food, water, and waste on another, Noah's family with possibly some smaller animals or domesticated animals on a third. Someone postulated for stability the heaviest loads would have been on the bottom floor. This makes perfect engineering sense.

Many see typology with this construction. Formed wood equals the cross, as does the pitch. The window equals the Spirit and/or prayer. The door equals Jesus, as He said He was the Door. The three floors equal repent, water baptism, and Spirit baptism. Faith means getting on the ark, or even building it before rain ever existed. God's mercy lasted centuries in this time-period. And Noah had to get in the ark, leaving brothers, sisters, and others behind.

Genesis 6:17 "And, behold, I, even I, do bring a flood of waters upon the earth, to destroy all flesh, wherein is the breath of life, from under heaven; and every thing that is in the earth shall die."

Everything that had the breath of life shall die. Unless it was in the ark. The whole creation currently waits for the manifestation of the sons of God. Why? When mankind fell, creation was cursed. When man is ultimately saved, creation will be blessed.

God pronounces that it is "I, even I." No one else is making this decision. There are no Watchers helping. God Himself is taking full responsibility for cleansing the world of every man, woman, child, animal, and plant life from the face of the earth. Notice again everything in the earth shall die. This is continually emphasized, that this is not a localized phenomenon. This is worldwide. Everything under heaven. Bacteria and microbes would have been on the ark or preserved in the water or on the floating plants. But all organic material died that was not on the ark, everywhere in the world.

Death. The final culmination of Adam's sinful disobedience. After 1600 years or so, everything will perish but a chosen few. Houses, cities, everything manmade will be destroyed. One sin led to billions of human deaths, and unto trillions of other living things. Every thing in the Earth as this passage says. The Earth would be purged from sin. Just as baptism cleanses us (1 Peter 3:20, 21).

Demonic spirits are here excluded in the destruction. Only things wherein is the breath of life are included.

Genesis 6:18 "But with thee will I establish my covenant; and thou shalt come into the ark, thou, and thy sons, and thy wife, and thy sons' wives with thee."

This is the first mention of covenant in Scripture. We speak of the Adamic covenant and the Edenic covenant, but in Scripture, this is the first mention. And it is with Noah. Notice the singular "thee." This is not with Noah's sons and family, but with Noah alone. I am reminded of 1 Corinthians 7:14 which reads, "For the unbelieving husband is sanctified by the wife, and the unbelieving wife is sanctified by the husband: else were your children unclean; but now are they holy." This is not to imply Mrs. Noah was unholy. It is to say that the righteousness of a man can reverberate through time and family. Solomon was blessed because of David. Jacob was blessed because of Abraham, and we are as well. Righteousness echoes in ways only God fully knows. Proverbs 11:10 reminds us, "When it goeth well with the righteous, the city rejoiceth: and when the wicked perish, there is shouting."

Notice the use of the word "I." Just as God used it to signify His responsibility in judgment, it is also used to show the establishment of His covenant. It is His covenant, not Noah's. He sovereignly chooses to make it, but of course it was predicated on Noah's walk with God. So, God goes from explaining the building of the ark and the destruction that is coming, to showing the purpose of the ark, and its inhabitants. Its occupants would be family, eight, to be exact. We do not know why Noah's children did not have children before the Flood. It does remind us of Jesus' words of woe to them with child and those that give suck in those days of judgment and tribulation. Maybe God planned it that way. Also, with eight, this puts the speculation of Ham's wife being pregnant with some corrupt antediluvian seed.

The babe in the womb would have made nine.

Genesis 6:19 "And of every living thing of all flesh, two of every sort shalt thou bring into the ark, to keep them alive with thee; they shall be male and female."

It is wise to compare Scripture with Scripture. If we were to stop here, we would think that Noah had just two of every sort of animal with him in the ark. But in Chapter 7, this is expanded to show that yes, they came by twos. But there were three sets of twos of the clean animals, and one for sacrifice, and only two of the unclean. In Jesus' Ministry, sometimes you may have one donkey or two, one blind or two, one demoniac or two. But comparing Scripture with Scripture clarifies the meaning and situation.

Male and female, obviously for procreation. And every kind. Willmington has definitely shown that all known species could comfortably fit on the ark, even with the ark being measured with a small cubit. The ark would have at minimum a capacity of 500+ railroad cars, and the animals required would fit into about 110 railroad cars.

We notice it also says "thou shalt bring into the ark." When the time comes, God drew these animals to the ark. Where God guides, He provides, where He leads, He feeds. "Every sort" would be congruent with the "kinds" of Genesis 1.

Genesis 6:20 "Of fowls after their kind, and of cattle after their kind, of every creeping thing of the earth after his kind, two of every sort shall come unto thee, to keep them alive."

Birds could not just sit on the outside of the ark. The rain would have been too vehement. They were within. Now we get introduced to God's methodology for saving the animals. He would bring them to Noah. Just as animals were created with a migratory instinct, here the great Creator causes them to come to Noah from wherever in the world they were located. And God chose which ones. Possibly the healthiest to preserve DNA. And the purpose was re-emphasized, to keep them alive. So, death would reign to everything outside the ark, and life to everything within the ark. Nothing died in the ark for the entire duration of the voyage and beyond. No disease became rampant on board the ark. There was protection in the ark. In the ark, life. Without the ark, death. As in Adam, all die, so in Christ all are made alive.

Genesis 6:21 "And take thou unto thee of all food that is eaten, and thou shalt gather it to thee; and it shall be for food for thee, and for them."

Noah was not only to build the ark, but to gather food for the voyage. And all types of food. This would serve as a preservative. Maybe acorns and pinecones and the like, and this would help to preserve these among the plants, vegetation, and trees after the Flood. But of course, the primary purpose would be for food. So, God did not cause a complete sleep to come on the animals in the ark. They did eat. And if they ate, they did have waste, we would presume. And that could be quite a smell, and much work for the assembled crew of the ark in feeding and cleaning. But it was still infinitely better than being outside the ark. Eternally better as a matter of fact. So, the animals would come to Noah, but he would have to gather the food.

Genesis 6:22 "Thus did Noah; according to all that God commanded him, so did he."

Keeping all of God's commands is so important. Adam did not.

We have no prerogative to rebel against Deity. Saul was arbitrary, expecting that a large percentage of obedience would suffice. But 95% obedience is disobedience. We must be zealous to do all that God has said. We should seek and keep all His commands (1 Chronicles 28:6). Noah did it. Faith without works is dead. Noah without the ark is dead.

God is a God of precision. We see this in the created order. If things in every realm of existence are slightly out of order, then life becomes impossible. So it is with God's plan of salvation. Sincerity is not the plan of salvation. Ignorance is not the plan of salvation. The Gospel of Jesus Christ is, as expressed in Acts 2:38. Galatians was written in part to show how a little leaven leavens the whole lump. Adding circumcision to the Gospel is another Gospel entirely (Galatians 1:8, 9). It is His Gospel, He paid for it, and it is effectual. Why would we want another?

Chapter 7

HERE WE SEE THE GREATEST cataclysmic disaster after the Fall that has yet befallen man. Billions die. Animals die. Plant life dies. A world groans. But is made clean to start again by the mercies of God. Within seven chapters of the Bible's beginning, we have Paradise made, Paradise lost, a plan laid to regain it, and God repenting He had made man. And then billions more die in God's sovereign choice of judgment. All that was created in Chapters 1 and 2 on the earth are destroyed. Sin kills. Sin destroys. God will start the process over. And it will culminate with His coming.

Genesis 7:1 "And the LORD said unto Noah, Come thou and all thy house into the ark; for thee have I seen righteous before me in this generation."

Jehovah speaks to His preacher. He spoke much to Noah, like He did to Abram and Moses. "Come" is the word spoken. This is Jehovah's embrace. Come unto me all ye that labour and are heavy laden, and I will give you rest unto your souls. Come, drink of the waters of life freely. God's invitation is still to "come." And it is not just to Noah, but to all his house. God saw him righteous in that sin-perverted generation. One of the great lessons of Scripture is learning to live for God in the midst of a crooked generation. Noah was unbowable, he would not bow to the sin around him. He continued to walk with God like his great-grandfather Enoch. Every generation needs people who will not bow to the world but shine as lights. Nan Pamer's book "I Will Not Bow" should be required reading.

1 Peter 3:20 reads, "Which sometime were disobedient, when once the longsuffering of God waited in the days of Noah, while the ark was a preparing, wherein few, that is, eight souls were saved by water." Noah's preaching, and the century it took to build the ark, was God's longsuffering.

Noah's command had been to build an ark. As such, he could not go into all the world probably and preach of the impending judgment coming. He would have to stay near the ark and build, unless he had his family do that work.

What a difference a few feet make. Outside the ark, eternal death. A few feet away, on the other side of the boards and pitch, is life.

Genesis 7:2 "Of every clean beast thou shalt take to thee by sevens, the male and his female: and of beasts that are not clean by two, the male and his female."

Clean beasts must have been understood, even though Scripture does not declare how at this time. This is not a Mosaic designation that is around 900 years away. This was something that was obviously known to the Antediluvians. The assumption is that it was something that Adam understood, and he knew what beasts God would accept in sacrifice, and which ones He would not. And he shared this information with the pre-Flood world, or at least part of them. God would give the clean beasts a head-start in the post-Flood world. A three-to-one advantage. And of course, one clean beast to sacrifice. This understanding of the clean beasts is a great lesson in Biblical interpretation. There are some things the Bible assumes but does not say. Sacrifices are included in this as well. But we cannot go too deeply down that road, lest we make up possible fictitious things in Scripture. It is when Scripture reveals certain items, then deductions can be made. Tithe is another subject like that in Genesis 14 and 28 with Abram and Jacob.

Another example would be the life of Jesus. The Bible never says what Jesus did when He was 18. But just because the Scripture is silent, it does not mean that Jesus was never 18. The Bible may not mention how Jesus went from one city to another. Or that He slept most nights. Or many such things. But we know they occurred.

Genesis 7:3 "Of fowls also of the air by sevens, the male and the female; to keep seed alive upon the face of all the earth."

Here all fowls are seen to be clean, it appears. Later in the time of Moses not all fowl are clean. Why the difference? Possibly the eating of carcasses after the Flood, but I am certainly not sure of that. Or maybe it is an assumption that fowls are included with the clean animals. Whatever the case, all were to come into the ark. Dodo birds, Pterodactyl's and Archaeopteryx included. And we see God created the world to be inhabited.

Genesis 7:4 "For yet seven days, and I will cause it to rain upon the earth forty days and forty nights; and every living substance that I have made will I destroy from off the face of the earth."

Judgment is coming in seven days. Rain, which possibly had never fallen before, would be coming. And everything that God created and made would be destroyed. Water is a purifying agent. It would judge and cleanse. The Red Sea judged the Egyptians but made the Israelites to escape. Baptism cleanses us but judges and washes away our sins. God is not against breaking the marred vessel to remake it. Ussher puts this verse as the 10th day of the second month, or Sunday November 30th, 2349 BC, 2365 Julian Period, or 1656 anno mundi. Sounds good to me. God so loved the world. But sin had marred it. It was beyond the pale. Judgment must come. His holiness and love worked in tandem.

If you were on earth, the cursed earth, you died. If you listened to the preacher of righteousness, Noah, you lived. It was simple then. It is simple now.

Some say the rain would come from breaking up a water canopy upon the Earth that ferreted out harmful UV rays, contributing to longevity before the Flood. The water canopy would have had to have been transparent however, if the Sun, moon, and stars were given for signs and to be for visible. God could have just caused supernatural rain, just as He caused supernatural destruction on Sodom and Gomorrah and rained down hail in Joshua's campaign. There need be no natural explanation. So, in seven chapters we go from Paradise to Judgment. Rebellion even with the flaming sword and Eden being visible. With only two generations from Paradise until now, from Adam to Methuselah, and Methuselah to the Flood. Human nature, when unleashed, is terrible. The classic book "Lord of the Flies" shows us this, but so do the horrific massacres and tortures perpetuated throughout human history. And we also notice once again the universality of the Flood. This is no local judgment, but a worldwide Flood.

Genesis 7:5 "And Noah did according unto all that the LORD commanded him."

"All" is the focal point here. It is the key component. Most everyone does some of what God commands and expects. Many may do most. This is imprinted on us with conscience, natural law, God's Spirit wooing us, and the created order. But God expects total obedience. Saul did a lot of what God required, but God wanted all. 1 Chronicles 28:6 speaks of keeping and seeking all of God's commandments. Ignorance is no excuse. Following sincerely and earnestly will lead to the revelation of all. All takes effort. It takes a conscious exercise of the will. It takes the help and grace of God. And because Noah obeyed, his family was blessed. The world was saved to repopulate again. A little light dispels much darkness.

Faith without works is dead. Noah without the ark is dead. Show me thy faith without thy works, and I will shew thee my faith by my works. Works do not save us. Only God can save us. But saving faith will have a response.

Genesis 7:6 "And Noah was six hundred years old when the flood of waters was upon the earth."

Contrasting this verse with 5:32, and we find that 100 years had passed. Depending on your interpretation of 6:3, 120 years may have eclipsed. Noah only had three sons by the time he was 600. This may indicate that DNA had begun to degrade. We find later in Genesis that Sarah, Rebekah, and Rachel had difficulty in bearing children. God's Divine mercy may have been involved in Noah's paucity of children. If only Shem, Ham, and Japheth would be saved, why have Noah suffer with the thought of his children dying in the Flood? He would already have brothers and sisters perish in the cataclysm. In Genesis 9:1 it is indicated that Noah would be fruitful after the Flood in the bearing of children. Shem, Ham, and Japheth had no offspring before the Flood, only afterwards, as recorded in Genesis 10.

Genesis 7:7 "And Noah went in, and his sons, and his wife, and his sons' wives with him, into the ark, because of the waters of the flood. "

"Because" obviously means in anticipation of the flood here. We do not know how old Mrs. Noah was, nor the son's wives. Imagine going into this black hulking ship, being told of an impending doom that they had never witnessed before. The animal's supernatural march to the ark, much like a migratory instinct activated by God, must have greatly reassured the family. Ventilation would have been in the ship, and with ventilation, also light, but the overwhelming status on the ship would have been relative darkness. Possibly they had means for torches. Technology would have probably been much greater than we often give them credit for.

The contrast between the uncomplaining crew and other personages of the Pentateuch is telling. Lot's wife looked back, but not this crew. Israel wanted to go back to Egypt. This crew went forward. Unnamed faithful, that is what the ladies on this crew were. It had faithful Enoch in their heritage.

Genesis 7:8 "Of clean beasts, and of beasts that are not clean, and of fowls, and of every thing that creepeth upon the earth,"

Everything went in. Let us examine some of the animals. Condors, earthworms, giant sea turtles, stegosaurus, triceratops, TRex, Pterodactyl, Sabretooths, Wooly Mammoths, sloths, anteaters, skunks, skinks, alligators, crocodiles, butterflies, roaches, ants, spiders, granddaddy long legs, bees, wasps, mosquitoes, hornets, tigers, lions, rhino's, porcupines, wolverines, wolves, possums and others. The list is quite diverse and much longer than this. But all had to be on the ark to be saved. One can see, when it is considered, why so many think this is allegorical or a fanciful tale. But to Bible believers, we accept it by faith. But we also see the evidence and possibilities for it as well.

Genesis 7:9 "There went in two and two unto Noah into the ark, the male and the female, as God had commanded Noah."

We know that the clean had seven and the unclean two, but this does not preclude the entire procession being two by two. The seventh animal of each could have went with another of a different kind. God's grace is here seen. God did what Noah could not do, and that is collect every animal and insect on earth in the required strictures. If man was vegetarian before the Flood, I am sure this included animals as well. Paul said meats for the belly and the belly for meats. Man was created to eat meat. And animals were created to be eaten. But not yet.

Genesis 7:10 "And it came to pass after seven days, that the waters of the flood were upon the earth."

This process took seven days. Everything gets in the ark and prepared. You would think that the gathering of animals from all over the world would awaken people's attention. But sin had them in its grip. Signs were no match to sin. Maybe everyone had moved away from Noah because they did not want to hear him preach any longer. Possibly animals lived in very close proximity since they were not predators per se at this time. But the plan of salvation was there. The preacher was there. The miracles were there. But no converts but his family. Francis of Assisi would have been proud at the salvation of the animals.

Ussher once again puts it like this. On Sunday November 30th, 2349 BC God commands Noah into the Ark. On Sunday December 7th, the Flood begins. The world would never be the same. This new world, with the wickedness cleansed by water, would be obviously fascinating and exhilarating for Noah and his family. But might there have been a sense of sadness for the billions that were dead of all species? We will know later.

Genesis 7:11 "In the six hundredth year of Noah's life, in the second month, the seventeenth day of the month, the same day were all the fountains of the great deep broken up, and the windows of heaven were opened."

When the Russians drilled the deepest hole in the world in the 1970's, some 7.5 miles underground, they discovered water. Scientists at that point had thought that was impossible. We now know that there is three times the amount of water under the earth than there is above the earth. Evidently before the Flood, there was an even greater quantity of water beneath the earth. When the water accelerated upward, it came with such force, that this is in all probability where meteors and comets came from. Possibly even moons in our solar system, at least some of them, began with the force of the waters under the earth ascending. Certainly, this must have been an incredible amount of water.

But water also came from heaven. The windows of heaven were opened. In Genesis 1, there were waters above the firmament. Now these waters came down. Some have speculated that the waters were either salt or fresh water. There are interesting theories on both. The salt water was water of judgment. Or the earth was cursed with salt water at the Fall, and the fresh waters are waters from the Flood. I am officially neutral.

Some see a type of the New Birth here. When we break up our waters inside, and let the tears flow in repentance, God opens the windows of heaven and pours the Holy Ghost upon us. We came from the earth, so this type likens earth to us. And also out of our belly shall flow rivers of living water. Of course, Noah's Flood is likened to baptism (1 Peter 3:20).

Some have tried to estimate how much water it would take to cover the earth during the Flood. Skeptics have at times said that it would be impossible to have that much water. A few things to keep in mind: First, this could have been supernatural water from heaven. Secondly, we do not know how much water was created under the earth. Present calculations would have no bearing on Antediluvian realities. Third, many speculate during the great upheavals of the Flood, hills and mountains grew larger during the cataclysm, or were created at that time, or soon thereafter. There seems to be some evidence for this, but I have not studied it enough to be conclusive on this matter.

Another objection to Noah's survival on board the ark, is the fact that if the ark was 30,000 feet above land, the atmosphere would have been too thin for breathing to take place aboard the ark, and it would have been dangerously cold. Notice however, when we talk about these measurements, we talk about sea level. The barometric pressure and auxiliary functions would be normal, as the ark would be at sea level throughout the Flood.

Another thought to ponder: The same windows that bring blessing in Malachi 3, bring judgment here.

Genesis 7:12 "And the rain was upon the earth forty days and forty nights."

What a deluge this must have been. Fossils of fish, eating other fish being formed at this time. Mammoths and Sabretooths being frozen with flowers still undigested in their stomachs, showing the northern latitudes were once temperate, as well as the rapidity of the Flood event.

I am still fascinated by the symbiosis that must have been taking place in the ark. Did God give supernatural peace to the boat in the midst of the storm? How badly did it toss? It must have been exceedingly well-built to endure the sheets of rain pummeling it for

40 days, as well as the enormous waves. God must have guided the ark to miss the projectiles shooting up from the great deep. What was the economy like in the ark? Did the animals bellow? Seasickness? Waste removal? Someone said that a suction hole could have been in the bottom of the ark for the elimination of waste. I have no idea. Certainly, there would have been circulation necessary within the confines of the ark. And did Noah's family think of the horrific judgment outside? How often?

Outside the ark, we have all types of animals buried together in high ground around the world, in Nebraska, for one example. And so many fossils are in the form of suffocation, with the bent back and upward tilt of the head. And land animals being found fossilized in the Ocean, which obviously would not occur under normal circumstances. Amber encasing insects is another proof of the Flood. Sin has an ugly price. And since man had great responsibility as the head of the food chain, so to speak, his federal headship brought judgment on the world.

What happened to the Garden of Eden? Possibly it was brought down to the center of the earth as paradise or taken up to Heaven. We do find the tree of life, possibly in Ezekiel, and certainly in Revelation, so it appears to have been rescued. The Tree of life appears to have maintained its potency even after the Fall, hence the guardian Cherubim. And lucifer does not want people to get to the life-saving tree.

Genesis 7:13 "In the selfsame day entered Noah, and Shem, and Ham, and Japheth, the sons of Noah, and Noah's wife, and the three wives of his sons with them, into the ark;"

Did this occur seven days prior, or on the day the Flood came? It could be the seven days prior is when Noah and his family first had access to the completed ark. And during the next seven days, the process of 1,000's of animals entering the ark took place. Or a day could be an elongated period of time, as it sometimes is in Scripture, but this seems unlikely in the context. But the key is, everything that was going to be saved was in the ark.

I do not think enough credit is given to the work Noah and his family put into the building of the ark. Without complaining. While preaching and making no converts. And the wholehearted obedience Noah had to God. If he would have missed anything in the ark, he was dead. He did his job completely. And he lived a holy life in the midst of a crooked generation.

Genesis 7:14 "They, and every beast after his kind, and all the cattle after their kind, and every creeping thing that creepeth upon the earth after his kind, and every fowl after his kind, every bird of every sort."

It has been accurately pointed out that "kinds" would be an overarching type of species. One archetypical pair of wolves would have been enough to produce ultimately every variation of dog in existence. Cows, the same thing. So, this would greatly reduce the number of animals needed to start the world over again after the Flood. God, I am assuming, supernaturally made it where the animals would survive and not be barren, if any supernatural power were needed in that regards. Cockroaches, Emus, and Ostriches, I am still fascinated at the variation of animals in the ark.

Genesis 7:15 "And they went in unto Noah into the ark, two and two of all flesh, wherein is the breath of life."

Salvation and regeneration. After worldwide judgment comes again millennia later, we look for a New Heavens and a New Earth wherein dwelleth righteousness. After the Flood, certainly there were dramatic changes upon the earth. And evidently the Flood washed away the curse from the earth. The ground would bring forth abundantly, even in places man was not.

The absurdity of a localized flood is again seen. If this were just a gigantic Ancient Near Eastern Flood, but not worldwide, what would be the purpose of the ark, and of bringing animals into it? Man, and animals could have just migrated to another place. But all flesh with the breath of life had representation on the ark. A close reading of the Text reveals that a universal Flood is the Author's intention to communicate.

Genesis 7:16 "And they that went in, went in male and female of all flesh, as God had commanded him: and the LORD shut him in."

"All" and "every" are emphasized in verses 14-16 indicating the enormity of the endeavor. And once again, Noah appears to be commended for doing what God had commanded him to do. This is love, keeping God's commands, according to John 14:15. This verse could be interpreted that each male of the species led the way, but that is a lesser interpretation. The "him" used twice in the latter part of the verse seems to clearly indicate Noah.

Jehovah shuts him in. God created an enclosed garden for man in Eden. Here God shuts man in. After sin in the Garden, God had shut him out. Here God shuts him in, and by default all the chosen representatives, in. Noah was sealed. How the ark door could have been hermetically sealed is a matter of discussion. How he could have shut it without supernatural help is a perplexity. If it was dozens of feet high, and coated within and without with pitch, God had to have shut him in and sealed him. This would be a type of being sealed in the New Testament sense quite possibly, as well. God opens, and no man shuts, and shuts, and no man opens. And how would it be opened after the Flood?

This was the only route of salvation. Noah did what he could do by God's grace, direction, and strength, then God did what Noah could not do in closing the door and bringing judgement. The power of one, in the man Noah is seen, as well as the power of righteousness in the midst of bad circumstances. One person standing for God is powerful. Daniel did it. Paul did it. David did it. The three Hebrew young men stood against an Empire. It is always right to do right, as my old Pastor used to say.

Genesis 7:17 "And the flood was forty days upon the earth; and the waters increased, and bare up the ark, and it was lift up above the earth."

The explosion of subterranean waters was not universal, or else the ark would have been destroyed. But as the waters relentlessly came from above and from below in belching torrents, the ark was lifted up above the earth. I am reminded of Jesus' words saying if I be lifted up, I will draw all men unto me. And as the serpent was lifted up in the wilderness. Salvation was being lifted on high. Caves could not save. Mountains and trees could not rescue. Sinners had fallen into the hands of an angry God. But on the other side of the coin, mercy, for those in the ark. And an opportunity for the earth to begin again. The inability of knowing for sure how high Mt. Everest was before and during the Flood, prevents one from determining exactly how much water was required to get 15 cubits above the tallest mountain. But regardless, the Creative God would have enough on hand. It was as if He was cleansing the filth of rebellion and sin from the world and beginning anew with the righteous. What a symbol of baptism.

Genesis 7:18 "And the waters prevailed, and were increased greatly upon the earth; and the ark went upon the face of the waters."

The same Gospel that saves also condemns those that reject it. The ark had rescued the saved, but the rest had been shut out. The waters prevailed. Terra firma was powerless. And just as the Spirit of God was on the face of the waters in Genesis 1:2, here another salvic vehicle was once again on the face of the waters, this monumental ark of Noah. 427 flood legends from around the world testify to this traumatic event upon the world (See James George Frazer's Folklore in the Old Testament). God's salvation plan protected from judgment. God truly knows how to deliver the righteous in the day of judgement.

It is here necessary to conclude for now our discussion of God's great Book. It has been a pleasure and a learning experience for me. I have noticed things heretofore overlooked in my personal journey through Scripture.

Discussing eternal subjects, and leading people in Truth to Jesus, is man's highest object.

A Few Things I Noticed in the First Seven Chapters of Genesis God created all life with the blessing to reproduce and multiply.

He was so good to Adam and Eve and weighted the entire affair in their favor. And even in rebellion and transgression, God showed mercy, grace, and kindness. I was overwhelmed with the evilness of mankind. But there was always a remnant calling on the name of the LORD, 7,000 not bowing the knee to Baal, as it were. And the wheels of God's judgment grind exceedingly slow sometimes, but they grind exceedingly fine.

www.ingramcontent.com/pod-product-compliance
Lightning Source LLC
Chambersburg PA
CBHW030151100526
44592CB00009B/220